INTRODUCING
Derrida

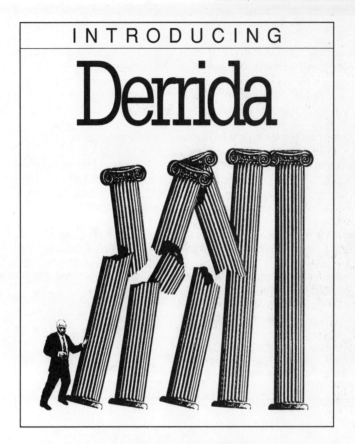

Jeff Collins and Bill Mayblin

Edited by Richard Appignanesi

ICON BOOKS UK   TOTEM BOOKS USA

This edition published in the UK in 2000
by Icon Books Ltd., Grange Road,
Duxford, Cambridge CB2 4QF
E-mail: info@iconbooks.co.uk
www.iconbooks.co.uk

Sold in the UK, Europe, South Africa
and Asia by Faber and Faber Ltd.,
3 Queen Square, London WC1N 3AU
or their agents

Distributed in the UK, Europe, South
Africa and Asia by TBS Ltd., Frating
Distribution Centre, Colchester Road,
Frating Green, Colchester CO7 7DW

This edition published in Australia
in 2000 by Allen & Unwin Pty. Ltd.,
PO Box 8500, 83 Alexander Street,
Crows Nest, NSW 2065

Previously published in the UK and
Australia in 1996 under the title
Derrida for Beginners

Reprinted 1998, 2001, 2002, 2003

First published in the USA in 1997
by Totem Books
Inquiries to: Icon Books Ltd.,
Grange Road, Duxford,
Cambridge CB2 4QF, UK

Reprinted in 1998

Distributed to the trade in the USA by
National Book Network Inc.,
4720 Boston Way, Lanham,
Maryland 20706

Distributed in Canada by
Penguin Books Canada,
10 Alcorn Avenue, Suite 300,
Toronto, Ontario M4V 3B2

ISBN 1 84046 118 7

Originating editor: Richard Appignanesi

Printed and bound in Australia
by McPherson's Printing Group, Victoria

Who is Derrida?

Jacques Derrida is a philosopher. Yet he's never written anything straightforwardly philosophical.

His work has been heralded as the most significant in contemporary thinking. But it's also been denounced as a corruption of all intellectual values.

Derrida has famously been associated with something called DECONSTRUCTION. Yet of all developments in contemporary philosophy, deconstruction might be the most difficult to summarize...

What Is Deconstruction?

There have been many answers.

a way of doing philosophy

a way of reading theoretical texts

a positive device for making trouble

not what you think it is

the latest fashion in literary theory

literature's revenge on philosophy

a traumatic response to philosophical certainties

an ancient error of scepticism and irrationalism

resistance to questions which begin "What is...?"

a repetition of dead-end themes in German idealism

a quasi-transcendentalism

a dangerous neo-Heideggerianism

an ethical response to conceptual complacency

a needless and frivolous hermeticism

a sustained assault on the Western philosophical tradition

All of these (and more) have been said of deconstruction. But there's some consensus on one point: its leading exponent has been Jacques Derrida.

Derrida's writing undermines our usual ideas about texts, meanings, concepts and identities – not just in philosophy, but in other fields as well.

Reactions to this have ranged from reasoned criticism to sheer abuse – deconstruction has been controversial. Should it be reviled as a politically pernicious nihilism, celebrated as a philosophy of radical choice and difference... or what?

There's much more to Derrida's work than the public controversies suggest. But controversy can reveal something about what's at stake in contemporary philosophy. A small quarrel at Cambridge has done precisely that...

BORDER LINES

According to a tradition dating from 1479, English universities award honorary degrees to distinguished people. It's never been quite clear why. But it's assumed that both parties benefit.

On 21 March 1992, senior members of the University of Cambridge gathered to decide its annual awards. It should have been a formality – no candidate had been opposed for twenty-nine years. But the name Jacques Derrida was on the list. Four of the dons ritually declared *non placet* ("not contented"). They were Dr Henry Erskine-Hill, Reader in Literary History; Ian Jack, Professor of English Literature; David Hugh Mellor, Professor of Philosophy; Raymond Ian Page, Bosworth Professor of Anglo-Saxon. And they forced the University to arrange a ballot.

There were two problems. First, this was a boundary dispute. Most of Derrida's proposers were members of the English faculty, but by training and profession Derrida is a philosopher. But more trenchantly, Cambridge traditionalists in both disciplines saw Derrida's thinking as deeply improper, offensive and subversive.

Campaigns were organized, and the Press was alerted. To the outraged dons, Derrida represented an insidious, fashionable strand of "French theory". They struck Anglo-Saxon attitudes...

FRENCH ACADEMIC PHILOSOPHY RUNS BY A SYSTEM OF MANDARINS AND GURUS AND FASHIONS. THEY WOULD BE GENERALLY PERCEIVED BY BRITISH PHILOSOPHERS AS NOT HAVING THE SAME STANDARDS OF PRECISION AND CLARITY AND RIGOUR WE WOULD. [David-Hillel Ruben]

LOTS OF PEOPLE THESE DAYS INVOKE SOMETHING CALLED "THEORY", WHICH I THINK A PROPER PHILOSOPHER WOULD NOT ADMIT TO. WHAT SORT OF WRITER IS DERRIDA? IS HE A FAILED THEORIST? IF NOT A THEORIST, THEN WHAT IS HE? [Henry Erskine-Hill]

THE FRENCH EXCEL IN FABRICATED TERMS OF SHIFTY MEANING WHICH MAKE IT IMPOSSIBLE TO DETECT AT WHAT POINT PHILOSOPHICAL SPECULATION TURNS TO GIBBERISH. DECONSTRUCTION IS A THEORY WHICH APPEARS TO LEND ITSELF MOST READILY TO BABBLING OBFUSCATION. [Peter Lennon]

There were political issues...

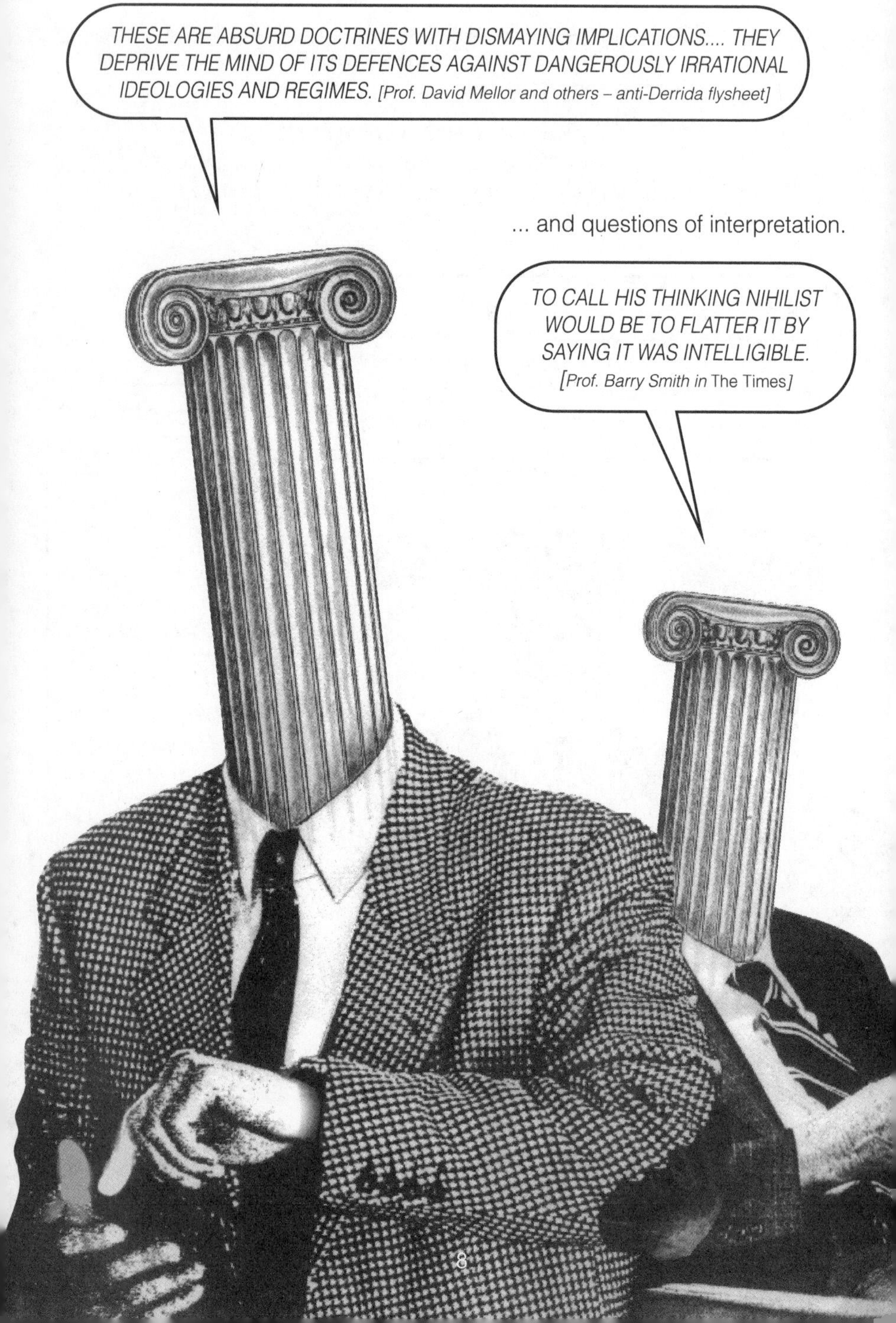

19 academics summed up the indictments in a letter to *The Times*:

Derrida Degree a Question of Honour

... M. Derrida describes himself as a philosopher. His influence, however, has been to a striking degree almost entirely in fields outside philosophy.

In the eyes of philosophers, and certainly those working in leading departments of philosophy throughout the world, M. Derrida's work does not meet accepted standards of clarity and rigour.

M. Derrida's writings seem to consist in no small part of elaborate jokes and puns. He seems to have come close to making a career out of translating into the academic sphere tricks and gimmicks similar to those of the Dadaists or the concrete poets.

Many French philosophers see in M. Derrida only cause for silent embarrassment, his antics having contributed significantly to the widespread impression that contemporary French philosophy is little more than an object of ridicule.

M. Derrida's voluminous writings in our view stretch the normal forms of academic scholarship beyond recognition.

Above all, his works employ a written style that defies comprehension. When the effort is made to penetrate it, it becomes clear that, where coherent assertions are being made at all, these are either false or trivial.

Barry Smith
(Editor, The Monist) and colleagues at the Internationale Akademie für Philosophie, Lichtenstein. May 6th. [signed by 18 others]

Derrida is accused of obfuscation, trickery and charlatanism. He's not a philosopher, he's a flim-flam artist. And strangely, his trivial joking gimmickry is seen as a powerful threat to philosophy – a corrosion in the very foundations of intellectual life.

But Derrida had his defenders, such as Jonathan Rée:
"The traditionalists were offering a mere and meagre argument from authority. They were refusing the possibility of dissent from established systems – an establishment stance, yes, but scarcely a philosophical stance..."

The ballot on 16 May vindicated Derrida and his supporters by 336 votes to 204. Derrida collected his award. But the dispute has continued.

O THE EDITOF

... To use mystification as a defensive weapon or as a cheap way of appearing 'deep' is still bad form. For all the intellectual brilliance of Derrida and others, their intellectual style corrupts and evidence of its corruption is to be seen in Anglo-Saxon academic life where post-structuralism and postmodernism have taken root.

PROF. R. A. SHARPE,
Dept of Philosophy
University of Wales

What was at stake? Underneath the posturing, there were two important questions:

The question of philosophy

Where and what are its boundaries? How are they produced and policed? What belongs "inside" philosophy, and what has to be expelled in the bid for "clarity and rigour"?

The question of philosophical language

What counts as a properly philosophical text? What form should it take? What kinds of language should it use?

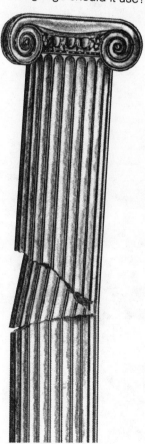

If the dons had wanted a rigorous address to these questions, they might have found one in the writings of a certain Jacques Derrida...

The Critique of Philosophy

Derrida's writing is a radical critique of philosophy. It questions the usual notions of *truth* and *knowledge.* It disrupts traditional ideas about *procedure* and *presentation.* And it questions the *authority* of philosophy.

*PHILOSOPHY IS FIRST AND FOREMOST **WRITING.** THEREFORE IT DEPENDS CRUCIALLY ON THE STYLES AND FORMS OF ITS LANGUAGE – FIGURES OF SPEECH, METAPHORS, EVEN LAYOUT ON THE PAGE. JUST AS **LITERATURE** DOES.*

So Derrida writes "philosophy" in something like "literary" ways. That's one reason for the anxieties at Cambridge. Derrida's critique of philosophy puts boundaries between philosophy and literature into question.

Derrida has destabilized other boundaries. He's taken his way of doing philosophy into art, architecture, law and politics. He's engaged with nuclear disarmament, racism, apartheid, feminist politics, the question of national identities, and other issues – including the authority of teaching institutions.

The profile of a joker? Perhaps, if we're willing to re-think joking ...

"Jacques Derrida"

By the time of the Cambridge dispute, Jacques Derrida's institutional credentials were internationally acknowledged.

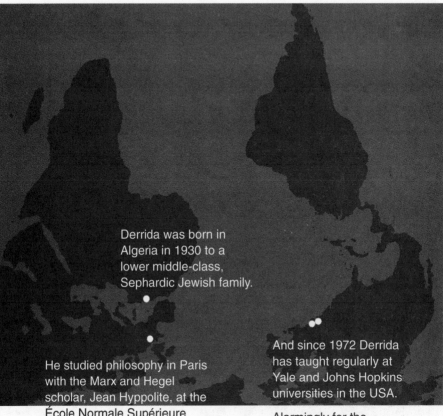

Derrida was born in Algeria in 1930 to a lower middle-class, Sephardic Jewish family.

He studied philosophy in Paris with the Marx and Hegel scholar, Jean Hyppolite, at the École Normale Supérieure (1952-6). His work on phenomenology was quickly recognized: a scholarship to Harvard in 1956, the Prix Cavaillès in 1962.

He taught philosophy at the Sorbonne (1960-4) and the École Normale Supérieure (1964-84). Since 1984, he's been Director of Studies at the École des Hautes Études en Sciences Sociales. These are well-founded institutions.

And since 1972 Derrida has taught regularly at Yale and Johns Hopkins universities in the USA.

Alarmingly for the Cambridge dons, his ideas were attractive. By the early 1980s, "Yale deconstruction" had introduced a wide Anglophone readership to the name Derrida, now one of the best-known names in international contemporary philosophy.

So Jacques Derrida is an establishment figure? Not entirely...

In 1957 Derrida planned a doctoral thesis on Husserl's phenomenology. But he abandoned it.

IS IT POSSIBLE TO WRITE ABOUT PHILOSOPHICAL WRITING WITHIN THE LIMITS OF AN ACADEMIC THESIS? WOULDN'T IT HAVE TO PERFORM WHAT IT ARGUED, AND THEREFORE HAVE TO BE WRITTEN DIFFERENTLY? WHAT IF THE EXAMINERS INSIST ON THE STANDARD PHILOSOPHICAL PROTOCOLS – THE ONES I WANT TO QUESTION?

Phenor

Psych

Philosop

Instead, Derrida embarked on a set of critical encounters with Western philosophy, literature and theory.

In **philosophy** this included German idealism (Kant and Hegel), phenomenology and its critics (Husserl, Heidegger and Lévinas), and the writings of Plato, Rousseau, Nietzsche and others.

Among **literary** writers, Mallarmé, Jabès, Artaud, Kafka, Joyce, Blanchot and Ponge figured prominently.

And between 1965 and 1972, Derrida was in contact with the *Tel Quel* group (Philippe Sollers, Julia Kristeva, Roland Barthes, and others). They debated **contemporary theory**, especially psychoanalysis, structuralism, and Marxism.

Reading Derrida's writing

Derrida's critique of philosophy is not a standard critique. It's not couched in the usual terms.

Derrida doesn't adopt any fixed *position* among competing tendencies and traditions. He doesn't simply *advocate* or *refute* any of them. And he doesn't advance any overarching *theories, concepts, methods* or *projects* of his own.

So Derrida's writing is impossible to summarize. In his terms it has no "basic" concepts or methods to pick out and explain. Yet it alludes constantly to a wide range of Western thinking. And it's often strategically convoluted. It disobeys the usual procedures – start at the beginning, lay out the exposition, advance the propositions, make a conclusion, etc.

The Cambridge dons were right. Derrida's writing is difficult and maybe subversive. It has a rigour and a logic, but of an unfamiliar order.

Is there a way of beginning to read this writing?

The Viral Matrix

If Derrida's writing has no extractable concepts·or method, we can still look at *what it does*: what *effects* it has.

Derrida offers a way of thinking these effects. By his own account, his writing has a matrix. Its two strands are DERAILED COMMUNICATION and UNDECIDABILITY. Derrida finds both of these in the figure of the **virus**.

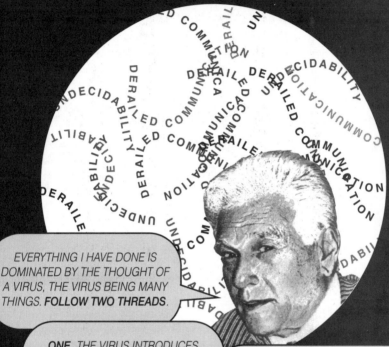

EVERYTHING I HAVE DONE IS DOMINATED BY THE THOUGHT OF A VIRUS, THE VIRUS BEING MANY THINGS. FOLLOW TWO THREADS.

ONE, THE VIRUS INTRODUCES DISORDER INTO COMMUNICATION, EVEN IN THE BIOLOGICAL SPHERE – A DERAILING OF CODING AND DECODING.

TWO, A VIRUS IS NOT A MICROBE, IT IS NEITHER LIVING NOR NON-LIVING, NEITHER ALIVE NOR DEAD. FOLLOW THESE THREADS AND YOU HAVE THE MATRIX OF ALL I HAVE DONE SINCE I STARTED WRITING.

We can take the second thread first: UNDECIDABILITY. If the virus is neither living *nor* non-living, then it's puzzlingly undecidable. As we'll see, undecidability is a threat to the traditional foundations of philosophy. But it's also a thread that can be picked up "outside" philosophy, in the cinema...

UNDECIDABILITY

The zombie is a late arrival in Western culture. It figures in the religion of enslaved West Africans in Haiti from the 17th century. For two hundred years Western colonialists pictured "voodoo" as a terrorist religion of blood sacrifices and cannibalistic atrocities.

But the zombie is a different kind of terror: a body without soul, mind, volition or speech. It's said to be a reactivated corpse, or a living body rendered soulless and mindless by sorcery.

Between Life and Death

The zombie entered Western popular culture in the late 1920s. *White Zombie*, 1932, set the formula for Hollywood: white science meets black magic.

It's an anxious encounter. What if the Western rationalist distinction of "life" and "death" doesn't hold?

The anxiety has taken many forms. Zombies have been cast as catatonic lovers, inner-city policemen, invaders from the stratosphere, military expeditionaries, night club entertainers, and so on.

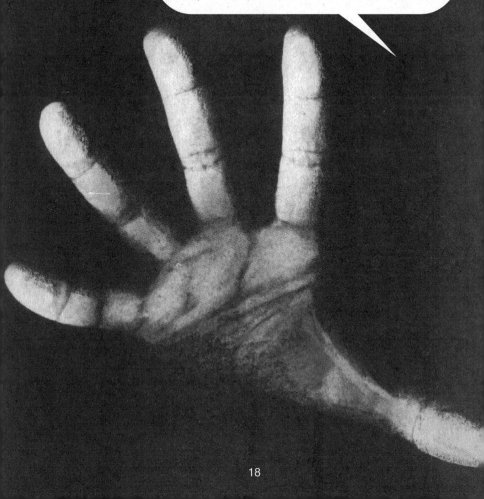

BUT WHATEVER THE SCENARIO, THE ZOMBIE HAS A BASIC MODEL: **ALIVE BUT DEAD, DEAD BUT ALIVE.** IN A CULTURE WHICH SEPARATES THE LIVING FROM THE DEAD, THE ZOMBIE OCCUPIES THE SPACE IN BETWEEN.

Between life and death – it's an uncertain space. The zombie might be EITHER alive OR dead. But it cuts across these categories: it is BOTH alive AND dead. Equally it is NEITHER alive NOR dead, since it cannot take on the "full" senses of these terms. True life must preclude true death. The zombie short-circuits the usual logic of distinction. Having both states, it has neither. It belongs to a different order of things: in terms of life and death, *it cannot be decided*.

According to Hollywood, the zombie is a "secret we must refuse to believe, even if it's true".

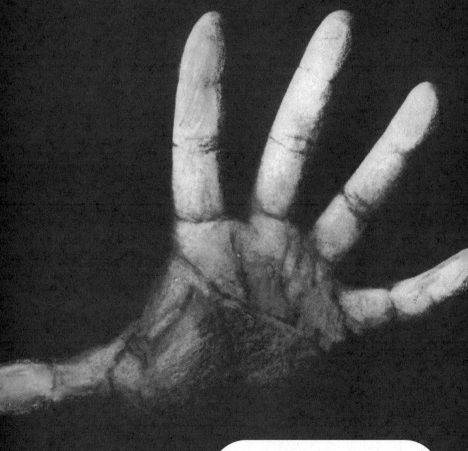

*UNDECIDABLES ARE **THREATENING**. THEY POISON THE COMFORTING SENSE THAT WE INHABIT A WORLD GOVERNED BY DECIDABLE CATEGORIES.*

Oppositions

The terms "life" and "death" form a BINARY OPPOSITION: a pair of contrasted terms, each of which depends on the other for its meaning. There are many such oppositions, and they're all governed by the distinction, **EITHER / OR.**

If we accept this, it establishes conceptual order. Binary oppositions classify and organize the objects, events and relations of the world. They make decision possible. And they govern thinking in everyday life, as well as philosophy, theory and the sciences.

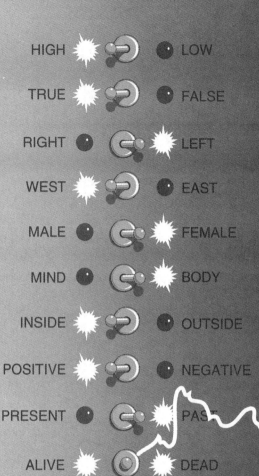

HIGH — LOW
TRUE — FALSE
RIGHT — LEFT
WEST — EAST
MALE — FEMALE
MIND — BODY
INSIDE — OUTSIDE
POSITIVE — NEGATIVE
PRESENT — PAST
ALIVE — DEAD

Undecidables disrupt this oppositional logic. They slip across both sides of an opposition but don't properly fit either. They are more than the opposition can allow. And because of that, they question the very principle of "opposition".

The Horror of Indeterminacy

Zombies are cinematic inscriptions of the failure of the "life/death" opposition. They show where classificatory order breaks down: they mark the limits of order.

Like all undecidables, zombies infect the oppositions grouped around them. These **ought** to establish stable, clear and permanent categories.

But what happens to "white/black", "master/servant", and "civilized/primitive", when white colonialists can also be the zombie slaves of a black power? Can "white science/black magic" remain untroubled, if what sometimes works against a zombie is *white magic* – the Christian religion, the power of love or superior morality? How certain is the opposition "inside/outside", if the zombie's internal soul is extracted and an external force becomes its inside? Is there any security in opposing "masculine" to "feminine" and "good" to "evil", when the zombie is usually de-sexualized and has no power of decision?

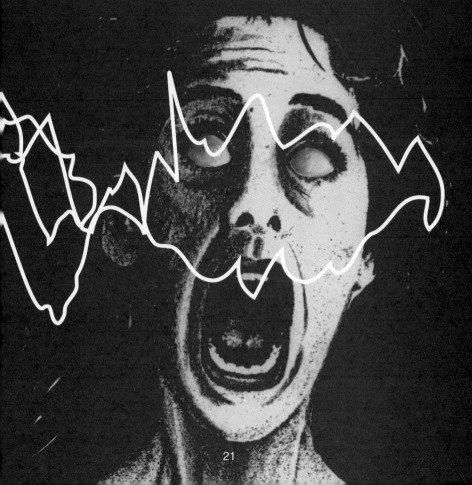

The zombie is therefore fascinating and also horrific. It poisons systems of order, and like all undecidables *ought* to be returned to order.

In zombie movies, this return to order is difficult. For a classic satisfying ending, the troubling element has to be removed, perhaps by killing it. But zombies are already dead (while alive). You can't kill a zombie, you have to resolve it. It has to be "killed" categorically, by removing its undecidability. A magic agent or superior power will have to *decide* the zombie, returning it to one side of the opposition or the other. It has to become a proper corpse or a true living being.

At that point the familiar concepts of life and death can rule again, untroubled. This is a restoration of conceptual order.

There are other endings, less final. The zombies might be ineradicable, they might return. Perhaps undecidability is always with us. If not figured in the zombie, then something else: ghosts, golems or vampires, between life and death. Between male and female, the androgyne. Between human and machine, the android. Between friends and enemies, the stranger...

Plato's Inauguration of Philosophy

Derrida argues that undecidability is a component of Western philosophy, but one which philosophy must refuse to recognize – or it will no longer be "philosophy" as we've known it. (It's a "truth we must refuse to believe"...)

Derrida detects the play of undecidability even in the foundational texts of the Western tradition, such as those of **Plato** (428-347 BC). Pupil of Socrates and founder of the Athenian Academy, writer on ethics, politics, law and metaphysics, Plato is an inaugural figure of Western philosophy, and widely influential on later thinking.

FOR ME, SOCRATIC REASONING IS THE ONLY TRUE ROUTE TO KNOWLEDGE.

Plato sets the love of reason and truth against all purveyors of false wisdom:- the sophists and rhetoricians, whose persuasive word-play deludes the untrained; and the poets, mythologists and story-tellers who merely imitate nature or "repeat-without-knowing". True philosophy is the active employment of reason.

How, then, does Derrida read Plato?

25

Plato's Pharmacy

In "Plato's Pharmacy" (1969) Derrida focusses on the *Phaedrus*, a fictionalized conversation between two historical characters: Socrates and Phaedrus, a young Athenian swayed by the rhetoricians. The topic: the relative merits of the lover and the non-lover, as sexual partners and as thinkers. Or perhaps the topic is the relative merits of rhetoric and philosophy (or perhaps, the merits of speech and writing).

SOCRATES   PHAEDRUS

MY CONCERN IS SPEECH AND WRITING. I EXAMINE THE SHORT FINAL SECTION IN WHICH SOCRATES (WHO NEVER WROTE ANYTHING) CONVINCES PHAEDRUS THAT SPEECH IS SUPERIOR TO WRITING...

IS WRITING SEEMLY? DOES THE WRITER CUT A RESPECTABLE FIGURE? IS IT PROPER TO WRITE? OF COURSE NOT. BUT SOCRATES IS NOT GOING TO USE RATIONAL ARGUMENT. MYTH WILL STRIKE THE FIRST BLOW...

AS FAR AS WORDS ARE CONCERNED, DO YOU KNOW WHAT WOULD MOST PLEASE THE GODS?

NO, I DON'T. DO YOU ?

WELL, I CAN TELL YOU WHAT I'VE HEARD FROM OUR PREDECESSORS ...

*... THEY SAY THAT THERE DWELT AT NAUCRATIS IN EGYPT ONE OF THE ANCIENT GODS OF THAT COUNTRY, AN INVENTOR-GOD WHOSE NAME WAS **THEUTH**.*

HE INVENTED NUMBERS AND CALCULATION AND GEOMETRY AND ASTRONOMY, AS WELL AS GAMES OF DRAUGHTS AND DICE, AND ABOVE ALL ...

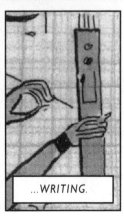

...WRITING.

AT THAT TIME THE GREAT GOD-KING OF ALL OF UPPER EGYPT WAS **THAMUS**. THE GREEKS CALL HIM AMMON. THEUTH CAME TO HIM AND EXHIBITED HIS INVENTIONS, SAYING THAT THEY OUGHT TO BE MADE KNOWN TO ALL THE EGYPTIANS....

HIS INVENTIONS WILL HAVE NO VALUE UNLESS GOD-THE-KING APPROVES OF THEM.

THAMUS INQUIRED INTO EACH ONE OF THEM, CONDEMNING SOME AND PRAISING OTHERS. IT WOULD TAKE TOO LONG TO GO THROUGH ALL OF THEM. BUT WHEN IT CAME TO **WRITING**....

THIS BRANCH OF LEARNING, MY LORD, WILL MAKE THE EGYPTIANS WISER AND IMPROVE THEIR MEMORIES, FOR I'VE DISCOVERED A **PHARMAKON** FOR MEMORY AND WISDOM.

Pharmakon is a Greek word which could be translated as "magic potion". Other English translations have used "recipe", "receipt", "specific", "cure" and "remedy". But as Derrida notes, *pharmakon* is a specially ambiguous word.

In Greek, *pharmakon* means both cure and poison. Like the English word "drug", it has good and bad aspects. Some translations resolve the word, cutting out one of its poles. But the *pharmakon* is UNDECIDABLE, inhabiting both the curative and the poisonous.

THEUTH HAS OFFERED WRITING AS A PHARMAKON. DOES HE MEAN "CURE"? SURELY HE WANTS TO WIN HIS CASE. WRITING IS A **REMEDY** FOR DEFICIENT MEMORY AND LIMITED WISDOM.

THE KING'S REPLY WILL BE INCISIVE...

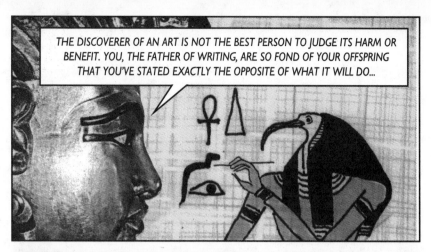

THE DISCOVERER OF AN ART IS NOT THE BEST PERSON TO JUDGE ITS HARM OR BENEFIT. YOU, THE FATHER OF WRITING, ARE SO FOND OF YOUR OFFSPRING THAT YOU'VE STATED EXACTLY THE OPPOSITE OF WHAT IT WILL DO...

THOSE WHO WRITE WILL STOP EXERCISING THEIR MEMORY AND BECOME FORGETFUL. THEY'LL RELY ON THE **EXTERNAL** MARKS OF WRITING INSTEAD OF THEIR **INTERNAL** CAPACITY TO REMEMBER THINGS. YOU'VE DISCOVERED A **PHARMAKON** FOR REMINDING, NOT FOR TRUE MEMORY...

AS FOR WISDOM, YOU OFFER YOUR STUDENTS A MERE **APPEARANCE** OF IT, NOT THE **REALITY.** THEY'LL RECEIVE MANY THINGS FROM YOU, BUT WITHOUT PROPER INSTRUCTION. THEY'LL SEEM KNOWLEDGEABLE WHEN THEY'RE QUITE IGNORANT. AND THEY'LL BE HARD TO GET ALONG WITH – THEY'LL CARRY THE CONCEIT OF WISDOM, INSTEAD OF BEING REALLY WISE.

WHAT YOUR THEBAN SAYS IS QUITE SOUND, I'M SURE.

LIKE PORTRAIT PAINTINGS, WRITING IS **LIFELESS**. IT CAN'T ANSWER BACK WHEN YOU ASK IT A QUESTION. AND WRITING CAN BE BANDIED AROUND ANYWHERE, AMONG THOSE WHO UNDERSTAND AND THOSE WHO HAVE NO BUSINESS WITH IT.

IT CANNOT KNOW WHO IT OUGHT TO SPEAK TO. WHEN IT'S UNFAIRLY ABUSED, IT NEEDS ITS FATHER THERE TO SUPPORT IT, BECAUSE IT'S QUITE INCAPABLE OF HELPING OR DEFENDING ITSELF.

WRITING IS CONDEMNED: REAL MEMORY WILL DECLINE, TRUE EDUCATION WILL BE CORRUPTED, FALSE KNOWLEDGE WILL REPLACE TRUE WISDOM. WRITING IS LIFELESS, ORPHANED AND HELPLESS.

But Theuth offered it as a *pharmakon*. Thamus, with all the authority of the king of kings and god of gods, returns it *decided*. **Writing is a poison!**

31

The Cure for Pharmaceuticals

Writing as an undecidable has been returned "decided". Derrida wants to keep it in play.

He shows how Plato's argument depends throughout on a set of simple, clear-cut oppositions:

good/evil,

inside/outside,

true/false,

essence/appearance,

life/death.

Plato's definition of writing is inserted into these oppositions. Speech is **good**, writing **bad**. True memory is **internal**, written reminding is **external**. Speech carries the **essence** of knowledge, writing its **appearance**. Spoken signs are **living**, written marks **lifeless**.

IF ONE GOT TO THINKING THAT SOMETHING LIKE THE **PHARMAKON** GOVERNED THESE OPPOSITIONS, ONE WOULD HAVE TO BEND INTO STRANGE CONTORTIONS WHAT COULD NO LONGER SIMPLY BE CALLED "LOGIC".

In Derrida's view, writing has characteristics that can't be decided within these oppositions. It disrupts the oppositions. It plays across good and bad, curative and injurious. There is neither simply cure nor simply poison. The characteristics of writing inhabit "interior" memory while also being "external". "Living" speech shares in the characteristics of "dead" writing. Writing refuses to settle down as the mere "appearance" of "true" knowledge.

Even Plato cannot avoid this. He resorts to metaphors of writing to describe "true" knowledge and "internal" memory.

THE ONLY SPEECHES THAT ARE WORTHY OF SERIOUS ATTENTION ARE THOSE THAT ARE TAUGHT AND SPOKEN FOR THE SAKE OF LEARNING, AND ACTUALLY **WRITTEN** IN THE SOUL.

WRITING AS **PHARMAKON** CANNOT BE FIXED DOWN WITHIN PLATO'S OPPOSITIONS. THE PHARMAKON HAS NO PROPER OR DETERMINATE CHARACTER. IT IS THE PLAY OF POSSIBILITIES, THE MOVEMENTS BACK AND FORTH, INTO AND OUT OF THE OPPOSITES.

The Supplement

Once the aberrant logic of the *pharmakon* is let loose, it poisons the fixity and clarity of the other oppositions grouped around it. For instance, Plato's argument relies on father/son, Egyptian/Greek, original/derivation. Can we be sure of these?

In Derrida's hands, they start to unravel. He turns to the "original" Egyptian myth where the characters are Thoth and King Ammon. Thoth is the son of the sun god, Ammon.

Derrida introduces the SUPPLEMENT. Thoth is the supplement to Ammon. The French word *supplément* means both addition and replacement. The supplement both extends and replaces – as a dietary supplement both adds to the diet and becomes part of the diet.

The supplement obeys a strange logic.

To be an addition means to be added to something already complete ...

... yet it cannot be complete if it needs an addition. The king is complete and has an addition; needing an addition, the king is not yet whole.

The supplement extends by repeating. The king's son has the same blood and is the king's extension. But the supplement opposes by replacing. The king's son will usurp the king, take his place.

The declaration, "The king is dead, long live the king!" must escape the grip of standard logic. It follows the logic of the supplement. The king must be *the same but different*: he is figured twice, as the father-king and the supplement-king.

So Thoth opposes his father-king, but he opposes what he himself repeats. He opposes himself. **Thoth, the demi-god, is undecidable**. And so is Theuth, his Greek counterpart...

The Joker

"Theuth is thus the father's other, the father, and himself. He cannot be assigned a fixed location in this play. Sly, slippery and masked, an intriguer and a card, he is neither king nor jack, but rather a sort of *joker*, a floating signifier, a wild card, one who puts play into play." And this joker is the inventor of play, of games of draughts, dice, etc.

Every act of his is marked by an unstable ambivalence. He is the god of calculation, arithmetic and rational science; and he also presides over the occult sciences, astrology and alchemy. He is the god of magic formulae, of secret accounts, of hidden texts. And so he is the god of *medicine.* The god of writing is the god of the *pharmakon*...

So can Theuth simply have meant writing as a "remedy"? Isn't the undecidable demi-god condemned to invent undecidables? Not just remedies, but *pharmakons*? And Derrida asks, "Isn't Theuth's desire for writing a desire for orphanhood and patricidal subversion? Isn't this *pharmakon* a criminal thing, a poisoned gift?"

Magician and Scapegoat

Plato's attempts to fix down fathers/sons and original/derivative are also attempts to fix down "philosophy". But philosophy has no easy remedy for undecidables. Derrida takes up some related words.

PHARMAKEUS, magician or sorcerer, is applied to Socrates himself by his accusers and enemies. Is Socrates working by *enchantment*? Is the sorcery of the undecidable *inside* philosophy, inescapably part of philosophical method?

PHARMAKOS means scapegoat. It's an evil found inside the city that must be cast out to maintain the city's purity. The scapegoat must belong to the inside, but must also belong to the outside. It's an undecidable. Writing is the undecidable *pharmakos* of philosophy. Found inside philosophy (Plato writes), it needs to be cast out (Plato condemns writing). Philosophy is set against itself.

"Inside/outside" assures us of order. On its assurance, Plato tells us what is properly "inside" philosophy. Derrida's strategies unfix the order.

This is not standard philosophical procedure. We'd expect a refutation of Plato or a confirmation: a clear agreement or disagreement. Or we'd expect the offer of "true" or "correct" meanings, or some explanation of Plato's "major concepts".

Such readings would reproduce Plato's logic: the attempt to master undecidability.

Instead of countering Plato's argument, or approving it or modifying it, Derrida insists on its instabilities. It is inhabited at every turn by an undecidability that it cannot fully master.

TO COME TO AN UNDERSTANDING WITH PLATO, IN THE WAY I'VE SKETCHED OUT, IS ALREADY TO SLIP AWAY FROM THE RECOGNIZED MODELS OF COMMENTARY, WHETHER THEY TRY TO CORROBORATE OR REFUTE, TO CONFIRM, OR TO OVERTURN, OR TO MARK A RETURN-TO-PLATO.

ISN'T THIS PLAY WITH WORDS, WITH THEIR LOCATIONS AND MEANINGS, MORE LIKE LITERARY CRITICISM OR COMPARATIVE MYTHOLOGY – OR SOMETHING ELSE?

Derrida does not so much explain Plato's text as "unfix" it. He sets its undecidables into unlikely movement.

Now from the perspectives of Plato's usual commentators, his operations seem open to the charges of the Cambridge professors: philosophically insignificant, lacking in rigour, contaminating, and so forth...

DERRIDA'S TEXT CANNOT BE EITHER IMPORTANT OR EVEN PROPERLY PHILOSOPHICAL.

DERRIDA IS TURNING ASIDE A SERIOUS PHILOSOPHICAL QUEST, DELIBERATELY PERVERTING IT. IT'S JUST A LITERARY-POETIC PLAY ON TURNS OF LANGUAGE.

SPEECH AND WRITING

Can Derrida's strategies be "important" to philosophy? Everything is against it. It's destined to *miss the point*, to pull Plato's text *outside* of philosophy, to *trivialize* Plato's thought.

But Derrida is confronting an argument for the priority of speech over writing. A side issue? According to Derrida, setting speech to rule over writing is crucial to the underpinning presuppositions of Western philosophy.

IF SO, TO UNDERMINE THE PRIVILEGE OF SPEECH IS ALSO TO UNDERMINE THE FOUNDATIONS OF WESTERN PHILOSOPHY.

This is a large claim. First, is it plausible?
Have philosophers privileged speech?

Phonocentrism

Derrida maintains that through three millenia of Western philosophy, from Plato and Aristotle to Rousseau, Hegel, Husserl and others, philosophers have indeed privileged speech.

What have they claimed?

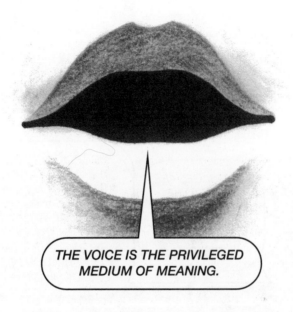

THE VOICE IS THE PRIVILEGED MEDIUM OF MEANING.

This is *phonocentrism*: the voice is the centre

Writing is derivative ...

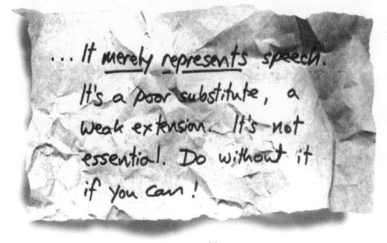

... It *merely represents* speech. It's a poor substitute, a weak extension. It's not essential. Do without it if you can!

If the voice is king, writing is its *enemy*. Writing is a pernicious threat to the true carrier of meaning.

If writing represents speech, speech is the representative of THOUGHT, of sovereign idea, of ideation, of consciousness itself.

 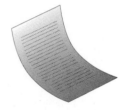

In the chain **thought** ....**speech**...**writing**,

speech lies closest to thought.

Aristotle of Stagira (384-322 BC), pupil of Plato and important source for Christian and Islamic philosophy.

Jean-Jacques Rousseau (1712-78), philosopher of nature and forerunner of Romanticism.

Ferdinand de Saussure (1857-1913), Swiss linguist and pioneer of structuralism and semiotics.

Is Writing Both Useless and Dangerous?

This doesn't square easily with the social history of the rise of writing in the West. Can we imagine capitalist economics, the power of the Christian Church, political systems, military structures, law, education, the arts, *without* records, books, writing? Literacy is the cornerstone of class education, safeguarded as the written and the readable, *not* the speakable and the audible.

Doesn't the history of the West in fact privilege *writing*?

The philosophers must be wrong. Have they fallen into avoidable error?

There *are* some arguments on their side. Sometimes speech *is* offered a curious privilege ...

LAW COURTS RELY ON WRITING, BUT WHAT DO THEY PRIVILEGE?... VOCAL TESTIMONY.

I PROMISE TO TELL THE TRUTH, THE WHOLE TRUTH, AND NOTHING BUT THE TRUTH

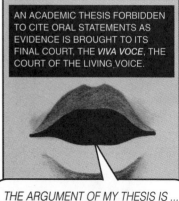

AN ACADEMIC THESIS FORBIDDEN TO CITE ORAL STATEMENTS AS EVIDENCE IS BROUGHT TO ITS FINAL COURT, THE *VIVA VOCE*, THE COURT OF THE LIVING VOICE.

THE ARGUMENT OF MY THESIS IS ...

THE MINUTES OF THE COMMITTEE MEETING ARE WRITTEN, BUT ARE RATIFIED AT THE NEXT MEETING IN SPEECH.

I CALL UPON THE SECRETARY TO READ THE MINUTES OF THE LAST MEETING

CAN A SHOPPING MALL BE PROPERLY OPENED EXCEPT BY SPEAKING WORDS?

I DECLARE THIS SHOPPING MALL "OPEN".

But that's not quite Derrida's argument. First, paradoxically, phonocentrism is a "history of silence", a repression of writing which can scarcely be acknowledged.

Secondly, the suppression of writing is *necessary* to Western philosophy, and all thinking influenced by it. It is crucial to philosophy's metaphysical presuppositions...

44

Metaphysics and Logocentrism

METAPHYSICS? BURN IT. NOTHING BUT SOPHISTRY AND ILLUSION.

Metaphysics inquires into aspects of reality which seem to lie beyond the empirically knowable world, out of reach of scientific methods. Its questions look like *the* philosophical questions: essential truth, being and knowing, mind, presence, time and space, causation, free will, belief in God, human immortality, etc.

Are there such questions? Empiricists like **David Hume** (1711-76), and many positivists, scientific naturalists, sceptics and others have said no.

But the questions persist. To set them up and answer them, Western metaphysics has looked for foundations:- fundamentals, principles, or a notion of the centre. These are the groundings for all of its inquiries and statements.

Logos (Greek) can mean logic, reason, the word, God.

This is the drive to ground truth in a single ultimate point – an ultimate *origin*. Derrida calls this impulse **logocentrism**. The *logos* is taken as the undivided point, the origin. Metaphysics ascribes **truth** to the *logos*, along with the origin of truth in general.

Metaphysics in its search for foundations is logocentric.

TRUTH

45

How Are the Foundations Laid?

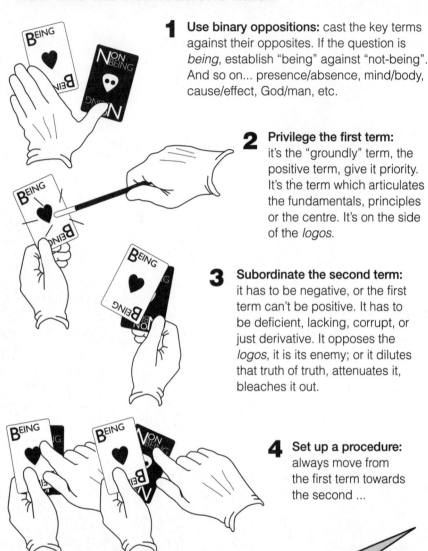

1 **Use binary oppositions:** cast the key terms against their opposites. If the question is *being*, establish "being" against "not-being". And so on... presence/absence, mind/body, cause/effect, God/man, etc.

2 **Privilege the first term:** it's the "groundly" term, the positive term, give it priority. It's the term which articulates the fundamentals, principles or the centre. It's on the side of the *logos*.

3 **Subordinate the second term:** it has to be negative, or the first term can't be positive. It has to be deficient, lacking, corrupt, or just derivative. It opposes the *logos*, it is its enemy; or it dilutes that truth of truth, attenuates it, bleaches it out.

4 **Set up a procedure:** always move from the first term towards the second ...

ALL METAPHYSICIANS PROCEED FROM AN ORIGIN, SEEN AS SIMPLE, INTACT, NORMAL, PURE, STANDARD, SELF-IDENTICAL ... TO TREAT THEN OF ACCIDENTS, DERIVATION, COMPLICATION, DETERIORATION. HENCE GOOD BEFORE EVIL, POSITIVE BEFORE NEGATIVE, PURE BEFORE IMPURE, SIMPLE BEFORE COMPLEX, ETC. THIS IS NOT JUST ONE METAPHYSICAL GESTURE AMONG OTHERS; IT IS THE METAPHYSICAL EXIGENCY, THE MOST CONSTANT, PROFOUND AND POTENT PROCEDURE.

Derrida and Metaphysics

Derrida's task is to undermine metaphysical thinking – to disrupt its foundations, dislodge its certitudes, turn aside its quests for an undivided point of origin, the *logos*.

It's a major task. Derrida argues that metaphysics *pervades* Western thought. In a sense, it has *been* Western thought. Is it escapable? Has anyone escaped it?

I HAVE SOME ALLIES – NIETZSCHE AND HEIDEGGER ESPECIALLY; MAYBE FREUD, SAUSSURE AND OTHERS. BUT EVEN IN THEM I READ A RESIDUAL **RELIANCE** ON METAPHYSICAL ASSUMPTIONS.

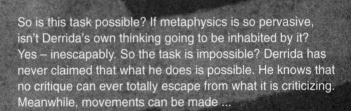

So is this task possible? If metaphysics is so pervasive, isn't Derrida's own thinking going to be inhabited by it? Yes – inescapably. So the task is impossible? Derrida has never claimed that what he does is possible. He knows that no critique can ever totally escape from what it is criticizing. Meanwhile, movements can be made ...

Overturning

It's always possible to OVERTURN a metaphysical binarism, to reverse its hierarchy by privileging its second term – for instance, to privilege body not mind, Man not God, the complex before the simple, absence rather than presence. Derrida does this. But ...

Displacement

Undecidability disrupts the binary structures of metaphysical thinking. It DISPLACES the "either/or" structure of oppositions. The undecidable plays all ways, takes no sides. It won't be fixed down. It leaves no certainty of privileged foundational term against subordinated second term. The unfixing of this certainty is the unfixing of metaphysics.

Derrida's philosophy has been called an anti-foundationalism. That's partly useful. But Derrida is not simply "against" foundations, he knows they're inescapable. However, metaphysical foundations can still be shaken. That's what he does. He makes a movement of *sollicitation* (French, from old Latin *sollicitare*, to shake as a whole), a shaking at the core, a tremor through the entire structure.

The Metaphysics of Presence

Metaphysical oppositions rely on assumptions of **presence**.

The first or privileged binary term carries "full" presence. Its subordinate is the term of **absence**, or of mediated, attenuated presence.

This is from **Martin Heidegger** (1889-1976), the German phenomenologist. Adopting Heidegger's formulation, Derrida argues that in Western thinking the *meaning of being* in general has been determined by *presence,* in all the senses of this word.

*PREOCCUPATION WITH THE QUESTION OF **BEING** LED ME TO REJECT MUCH OF TRADITIONAL METAPHYSICS.*

Presence can be **spatial**: e.g. proximity, nearness or adjacency, and also immediacy – having actual or direct contact, lacking mediation, having no intervening material, object or agency.

MY INTENTION IS TO MAKE ENIGMATIC WHAT ONE THINKS ONE UNDERSTANDS BY THESE WORDS.

And it can be **temporal**: it evokes the present as the single present moment, the *now*; and occurrence without delay, lapse or deferral .

Presence organizes metaphysical concepts of being. And all the "groundly" terms of metaphysics designate a presence. Derrida's examples ...

– presence of the object to sight

– presence as substance, essence or existence

– temporal presence as the point of the "now", or of the instant

– self-presence of thought or consciousness

– present being of the subject

– co-presence of the self and the other

> PRESENCE IS AT WORK THROUGHOUT WESTERN PHILOSOPHY – ALL THE EMPIRICISMS, IDEALISMS, RATIONALISMS, REALISMS, ETC. PSYCHOANALYSIS, PHENOMENOLOGY AND STRUCTURALISM HAVE NOT ESCAPED IT.

Presence is the foundation for many claims, philosophical or not:-

● that a truth can lie behind (therefore in proximity to) an appearance

● that there is an immediate bond between the "word of God" and truth

● that a "spirit of the age" can inform an historical era, and therefore be present within it

● that a photograph can capture the "significant moment", the now

● that an artist's expressed emotion can be present in their work

Presence and Speech

Why, then, is the speech/writing opposition so important? Why is the privileging of speech a gesture which *inaugurates* Western philosophy? And if philosophy as we know it is writing, why treat writing as a corruption, an obstacle or an irrelevance?

> BECAUSE IT'S A NECESSITY OF THE METAPHYSICS OF **PRESENCE**.

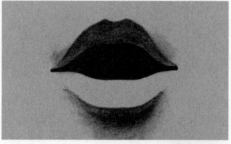

From that perspective...

Speech seems to carry full presence

Metaphysical concepts of being, in time and in space, demand presence.

Wish you were here.

Writing depends on absence

Its characteristics oppose presence. Metaphysical thinking has to eject it or subordinate it.

In speech, the speaker and the listener have to be *present* in at least two senses:-

A Present to the words in a spatial sense

B Present at a particular moment in time in which the words are uttered.

Therefore it seems that the speakers' *thoughts* are as close as possible to their *words*. The thoughts are *present* to the words. So speech offers the most direct access to consciousness. The voice can seem to *be* consciousness itself.

51

> When I speak, I am conscious of being present for what I think, but also of keeping as close as possible to my thought a signifying substance, a sound carried by my breath .... I hear this as soon as I emit it. It seems to depend only on my pure and free spontaneity, requiring the use of no instrument, no accessory, no force taken from the world. This signifying substance, this sound, seems to unite with my thought ... so that the sound seems to erase itself, become transparent .... allowing the concept to present itself as what it is, referring to nothing other than its presence.

Speech is transparent, a diaphanous veil through which we view consciousness. Speech and thought – nothing comes between them. No lapse of time, no surface, no gap.

So presence beguilingly seems to attend spoken words ...

BUT NOT WRITING.

Writing operates on absences. As Derrida indicates, it doesn't need the presence of the **writer**, or of the writer's consciousness.

"The written marks are abandoned, cut off from the writer, yet they continue to produce effects beyond his presence and beyond the present actuality of his meaning, i.e., beyond his life itself."

"To write is to produce a mark which will constitute a kind of machine that is in turn productive ... The writer's disappearance will not prevent it functioning."

And the same for the **reader**.

"All writing, in order to be what it is, must be able to function in the radical absence of every empirically determined addressee in general ... This is not a modification of presence, but a break in it, a 'death' or the possibility of a 'death' of the addressee."

Writing cannot be writing unless it can function in these two absences. Presence is unsustainable.

The Repression of Writing

The order of writing is distance, delay, opacity and ambiguity. And also death – "dead" meaning, not the living meaning of a present speaker. "Written words, in a state of defenceless misery" have to be "abandonable to their essential drifting."

So now we begin to understand the paradoxical phonocentric "history of silence", that repression of writing which can scarcely be acknowledged.

And it begins to explain the disturbing tactics of Derrida's own writing – its "difficulty".

The Agenda of the 1960s...

THE MOST STATIC PERIOD OF THE GAULLIST REPUBLIC

PHENOMENOLOGY VS. STRUCTURALISM

Derrida worked out the "speech/writing" problem across two dominant currents of French thinking: **phenomenology** and **structuralism**.

Phenomenology and structuralism are incompatible rivals – that was the prevailing view at the time. Let's look at these rivals.

First, what is PHENOMENOLOGY? A "philosophy of consciousness" – neither intellect nor science can grasp the fundamental nature of consciousness. To do this, philosophy has to deal with **phenomena** – appearances and our awareness of those appearances. This awareness can't be grasped through rational proofs and scientific data. What's needed is **intuition**, a direct approach to the inner structures of consciousness itself.

Some Key Phenomenologists

Edmund Husserl (1859-1938): mathematician seduced into philosophy, first phenomenologist, founder of the foundations; influential teacher at Göttingen 1901-16 and Freiburg 1916-28; visiting lecturer at the Sorbonne, Paris 1929.

Martin Heidegger (1889-1976): student of Husserl, successor to his chair in Philosophy at Freiburg.

Maurice Merleau-Ponty (1908-61): French philosopher, strongly influenced by Husserl in the 1930s.

BUT TO DESCRIBE THE FUNDAMENTAL EXPERIENCE OF THE WORLD NEEDS ATTENTION TO THE BODY, AND TO THE AMBIGUITIES OF EXPERIENCE. I FOUNDED THE EXISTENTIALIST JOURNAL "LES TEMPS MODERNES" WITH ...

FOR ME, PHENOMENOLOGY ISN'T A TOOL TO STUDY CONSCIOUSNESS. IT'S A MEANS OF REVISITING THE CENTRAL ONTOLOGICAL QUESTIONS:- THE HUMAN MODE OF BEING-IN-THE-WORLD, AND BEING ITSELF.

PHENOMENOLOGICAL REDUCTION EXPOSES THE ESSENTIAL ELEMENTS OF CONSCIOUSNESS.

Jean-Paul Sartre (1905-80): studied Husserl's work intensively in 1933-4. Through Sartre, phenomenology became the central platform for Existentialism, *the* philosophical vogue of the 40s and 50s.

I WAS NEVER IN DESPAIR

What is STRUCTURALISM? The study of human language, culture and society as **structures**. The elemental components of a structure are *related* to each other. So to analyze cooking (or economics, kinship, fashion, etc) examine its components in their **relationships** of difference, exchange, substitution. The ultimate model – language. Cultural and social structures work like language structures.

Some Key Structuralists

Ferdinand de Saussure (1857-1913): Swiss linguist, prototype structuralist. His posthumous *Course in General Linguistics* (1916) is about word-based signification.

Roman Jakobson (1896-1982): Russian-born "Prague Circle" linguist, Saussure's first major advocate.

I ADAPTED SAUSSURE'S CONCEPT OF LANGUAGE AND THE SIGN IN MY RADICAL RE-READING OF FREUD. THE UNCONSCIOUS IS STRUCTURED LIKE A LANGUAGE.

Louis Althusser (1918-90): philosopher and political theorist, structuralist reader of Marx.

Jacques Lacan (1901-81): psychoanalyst.

I TOOK STRUCTURAL LINGUISTICS TO AMERICA IN 1942, WHERE I MET....

Claude Lévi-Strauss (b. 1908): anthropologist, exponent of the structural study of culture, writer on kinship, myth, gift-exchange, etc.

BUT I ALSO PROPOSE THAT LANGUAGE STRUCTURES ARE THE BASIS FOR A SEMIOLOGY, A SCIENTIFIC STUDY OF SIGNS IN GENERAL.

CAPITALIST SOCIETIES ARE INTERACTIVE STRUCTURES, NOT EXPRESSIONS OR REFLECTIONS OF AN ECONOMIC BASE.

Roland Barthes (1915-80): literary critic and cultural theorist.

ON MY RETURN TO FRANCE IN 1949 I BECAME CENTRAL TO THE STRUCTURALISM OF THE 1950S AND 60S.

I READ SAUSSURE'S "COURSE" IN 1956 AND APPLIED ITS CONCEPTS TO LITERATURE, FASHION, ADVERTISING IMAGES, PHOTOGRAPHY, ETC.

There seemed to be irresolvable differences between phenomenology and structuralism.

They had different *projects*. Phenomenology is a philosophy of interior consciousness. Structuralism is a relational theory of language and culture.

And they had different conceptions of *meaning*. Meaning arises fundamentally in interior consciousness. Meaning arises in the relations between units of language.

But Derrida's aim has never been to *resolve* anything.

STRUCTURALISM

PHENOMENOLOGY

IF BOTH TENDENCIES RELY ON METAPHYSICAL ASSUMPTIONS, THEY'RE ALREADY MORE SIMILAR THAN DIFFERENT. SO I USE ASPECTS OF BOTH TO UNDERMINE THE FOUNDATIONS OF BOTH ...

Let's begin with phenomenology. Can we hold out the possibility of a pure consciousness at the level Husserl wanted? Derrida argues that such a possibility is excluded at the very root...

Ideas Proper to a Pure Phenomenology

In his quest for the fundamentals of consciousness, Husserl had to expel everything that was merely local or contingent. Anything that belonged to particular individuals or situations was a matter of individual psychology. The fundamental structures of the mind had to be universal, transcendent.

His strategies:

Phenomenological reduction: isolate the fundamental aspects by *bracketing out* everything else. Rigorous and meticulous elimination will yield an account of essential consciousness.

Reduce language ... or at least those aspects of it which can't be accommodated to pure consciousness. Bracket out the "exterior" aspects of language – all its apparatuses, forms, substances, sounds and marks.

Treat meaning as "interior" – it's a product of solitary mental life. Needing no exterior, fundamental meaning can only be a question of consciousness in communion with itself.

*AH, THIS IS MEANING **PRESENT TO ITSELF**. AT THE FOUNDATION OF THE UNIVERSAL STRUCTURE OF THE MIND, THE METAPHYSICS OF **PRESENCE**. AND THE WHOLE EDIFICE HAS TO RELY ON THE METAPHYSICAL OPPOSITION, INSIDE/OUTSIDE...*

For Husserl, is there any way of thinking the relation between thought and language? Yes. And it's governed by a binary opposition and a hierarchy.

The opposition: two kinds of sign:-
(a) EXPRESSIVE
(b) INDICATIVE

The hierarchy:-

The **EXPRESSIVE** sign is the properly meaningful sign, because it carries an intentional force, an *intention* to mean.

The **INDICATIVE** sign might signify, but it lacks this animating intention.

Examples of INDICATIVE signs:

Naturally occurring signs: the falling of leaves might signify "It is autumn". But leaves don't harbour intent.

Mathematical signs might be manipulated to signify arithmetically, geometrically, etc; but they need no active, current, semantic intention.

FOR HUSSERL, THIS IS AN "INFERIOR, DANGEROUS AND CRISIS-LADEN SYMBOLIZATION", BUT IT DOESN'T PREVENT MATHEMATICAL SIGNS FROM BEING PUT TO THEIR USES...

$2+2=4$

And the EXPRESSIVE sign?

If living intention is to animate it, it will need the presence of its living producer. So, what's the privileged form of the expressive sign? The speaking voice, superior to all other forms because it seems present (proximate, immediate) to the silent, interior consciousness. Husserl reproduces the phonocentric priority.

IN HUSSERL'S VIEW, TO EXPRESS ONESELF IS TO BE BEHIND THE SIGN ... TO ATTEND TO ONE'S SPEECH, TO ASSIST IT. ONLY LIVING SPEECH, IN ITS MASTERY AND MAGISTERIALITY, IS ABLE TO ASSIST ITSELF; AND ONLY LIVING SPEECH IS EXPRESSION AND NOT A SERVILE SIGN...

So what about the external supports of language – the marks, the sounds etc. which can be cut off from present intention, can go their own ways separately? To Derrida, these externals are always necessary and always inhabit the internal.

An encounter with Saussure's structuralist theory of language became inevitable.

Saussure's Linguistics

Saussure broke with previous approaches to linguistics. These had tracked the evolution of sounds and words across time. Saussure focussed on how language *worked*, not how it developed.

Language can be viewed **synchronically**, i.e., as if in a single moment. It can be seen as a structure or system, a set of elements located in *relation* to each other.

In structural linguistics, it's the play of those elements and relations which produces meaning. For Saussure, this happens in two ways.

FIRST, MEANING IS PRODUCED IN THE FORMATION OF SIGNS AS TWO-SIDED ENTITIES.

d/o/g =

SECOND, MEANING IS ALSO PRODUCED IN A PLAY OF DIFFERENCES.

FINE, LET'S LOOK AT THESE TWO CONCEPTS – THE SIGN AND DIFFERENCE.

The "sign" has two aspects:-

A signifier: for Saussure, this is a sensory perception (a spoken word has an aspect we can hear; a written word, an aspect we can see).

A signified: a concept or meaning associated with that sensory perception.

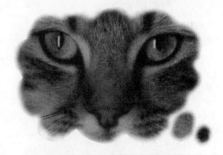

A sign, to be a sign, needs both aspects: something we **sense** and something we **think**. It's a relationship ...

This relationship is nothing new. It's the stock-in-trade of Western thinking about language. A sign has two aspects, one *sensible* and the other *intelligible*. Plato introduced the idea in his *Cratylus*, the Stoics formalized it, and it's passed into modern linguistics via early Christian thinkers and others.

A SIGN IS SOMETHING WHICH, IN ADDITION TO THE SUBSTANCE ABSORBED BY THE SENSES, CALLS TO MIND OF ITSELF SOME OTHER THING.

THE CONSTITUTIVE MARK OF EVERY SIGN IN GENERAL RESIDES IN ITS DOUBLE CHARACTER. IT IS BIPARTITE, AND HAS TWO ASPECTS: ONE SENSIBLE AND THE OTHER INTELLIGIBLE.

St Augustine (354-430)

Roman Jakobson (1896-1982)

To Derrida, this is suspect. The sign is premised on a binarism and it looks suspiciously like a foundational concept in Western thinking.

"The difference between signifier and signified is no doubt the governing pattern within which Platonism institutes itself as philosophy..."

But Saussure's sign might be useful to the critique of phenomenology. Especially, he emphasises that signifier and signified are indissolubly related. He insists that each requires the other – they cannot exist apart. Saussure conjures two metaphors. Signifier and signified are **body and soul**, or they are **recto and verso** of a leaf of paper. Saussure, choosing between them, prefers the sheet of paper. Its two sides are ultimately inseparable.

THE INVISIBLE, ALMOST NON-EXISTENT, THICKNESS OF THAT "LEAF" BETWEEN THE SIGNIFIER AND THE SIGNIFIED – A SIGNIFICANT METAPHOR, WE SHOULD NOTE, SINCE THE LEAF WITH ITS RECTO ...

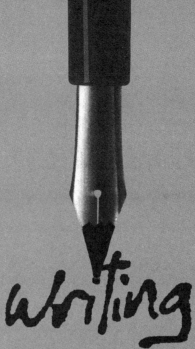

... AND VERSO FIRST APPEARS AS A SURFACE AND SUPPORT FOR

... *writing*

If Saussure is right, we can't be lured into the notion that concepts or meanings exist independently of signifiers. Concepts need their physical sounds, their scripted marks, etc. Even if we can imagine words "inside our head", we are conjuring their signifiers, their sensory aspects. Their external forms pollute the ideal of the purely internal.

So, for Derrida, this resists a classic move of Western metaphysics: the suppression of the signifier. The signified is the grounding term. The signifier? Inessential. It gets in the way, it corrupts the concept.

As with Husserl: evaporate the signifier and you're left with pure thought – a "transcendental signified". Where is this evaporation most complete? In the speaking voice, which seems to melt away under the force of the expressed consciousness.

But Saussure too falls back into this phonocentrism. What can be used to *displace* the sign?

Derrida uses Saussure's concept of **difference**.

Meaning can't be produced only in the binding of signifier to signified. It needs the operation of difference. How does this work, according to Saussure?

Saussure goes back to his "sheet of paper" metaphor.

If the sheet is cut into different shapes, one shape can be identified by its difference from the other shapes. That shape takes on an identity in relation to the others – it takes on a certain "value".

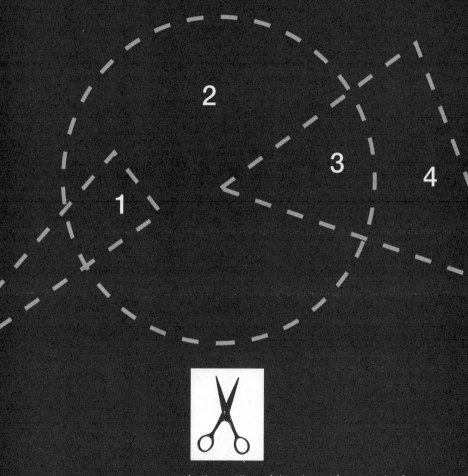

In the cutting of the sheet of paper, the front and back have to be cut at the same time. The different shapes of the "signifier" side ...

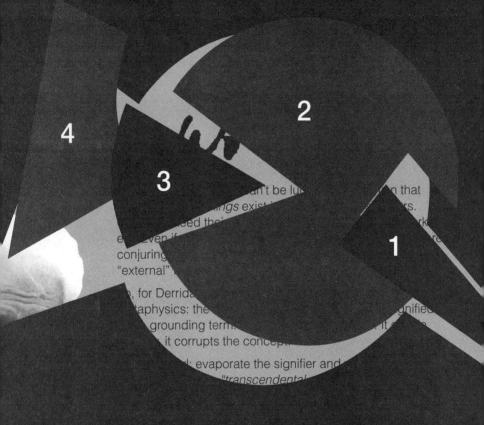

... make up the different shapes of the "signified" side. Signifiers *and* concepts are created in a system of differences.

From this comes Saussure's famous pronouncement – the structure of language is *purely* differential: "Whether we take the signified or the signifier, language has neither ideas nor sounds that existed *before* the linguistic system, but only conceptual and phonic differences that have issued *from* the system."

Meaning is no longer simply a correlation of signifier/signified. Everything depends on differences.

At the level of linguistic sounds, we can substitute the sound /**p**/ for the sound /**b**/ in *big*.

The sounds don't mean anything in themselves, but we can tell the difference between them. The difference makes possible a different meaning – the concept:

And so on, through other differentiable sounds and concepts:

peg

pen

pan

etc.

And for Derrida this is a question of presence...

What happens when *big* circulates as a spoken word? The sound /**b**/ has to be spoken. No /**p**/, it would seem, is present. We will not hear the /**p**/, a speaker cannot say one at the same time. We might say, it is absent. But on the other hand, /**p**/ is not simply absent. *Big*, to be identifiable and meaningful, depends on it, and on all the other sounds from which it differs. Without /**p**/ and the others, it is lost. So the /**p**/ is in a way present, though not simply so. It is carried as a *trace* in the /**b**/, necessarily present in its necessary absence.

The Trace

What does Derrida mean by "trace"? Neither simply present nor simply absent, the trace is an undecidable. The relay of differences (*pig, big, bag, rag, rat*, etc) depends upon a structural undecidability, a play of presence *and absence* at the origin of meaning. Undecidability at the "origin", *between* presence and absence.

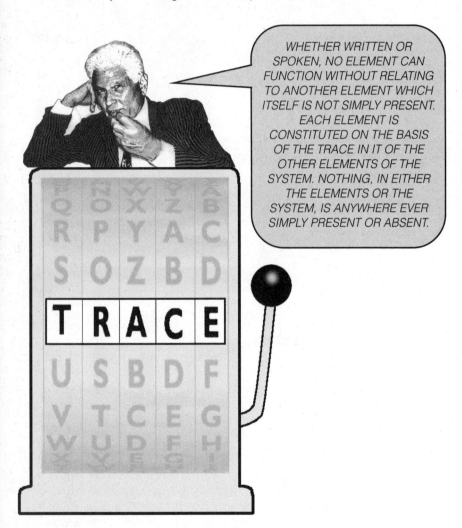

WHETHER WRITTEN OR SPOKEN, NO ELEMENT CAN FUNCTION WITHOUT RELATING TO ANOTHER ELEMENT WHICH ITSELF IS NOT SIMPLY PRESENT. EACH ELEMENT IS CONSTITUTED ON THE BASIS OF THE TRACE IN IT OF THE OTHER ELEMENTS OF THE SYSTEM. NOTHING, IN EITHER THE ELEMENTS OR THE SYSTEM, IS ANYWHERE EVER SIMPLY PRESENT OR ABSENT.

So Derrida sets the trace across the Saussurean sign – an undecidable presence-absence at the origin of meaning. Language is premised on an interweaving movement between what is there and not there. Language is always an interweaving, a textile.

What is the significance of Derrida's notion of the trace?

First, it suggests that all language is subject to undecidability. The play of the trace is a kind of deforming, reforming slippage – an inherent instability which language cannot escape.

This applies to philosophical language as well. The vocabulary of metaphysics (being, truth, centre, origin, etc) has to be recognized as a vocabulary. It's a set of words, and they cannot escape the play of the trace.

Now, if the trace is a constant sliding between presence and absence, those philosophical words cannot establish full, replete presence.

This strikes at the very roots of Western metaphysics, because it's the claim to full presence which underpins metaphysical concepts and procedures.

Structuralism and Phenomenology: Derrida's Operations

Derrida's writings on structuralism and phenomenology were published in 1967, in three books: *Speech and Phenomena*, *Writing and Difference*, and *Of Grammatology*. These were his first major publications, and they announced his complex assault on metaphysical thinking.

None of these texts offer arguments of the usual kind. They don't simply refute, corroborate, commend or oppose. Rather, Derrida "makes a passage through" the texts of phenomenology and structuralism, searching out their hidden points of instability – the points where undecidability is at work.

In a sense, Derrida does the same thing with phenomenology and structuralism that he does with Plato and others. Reading their texts, he finds undecidables: the *pharmakon,* the supplement, the trace, etc. And he uses the undecidables to shake up the metaphysical foundations.

This helps to explain why Derrida's writing can seem puzzling, infuriating or exasperating. To embrace the curious logic of this writing, we have to be willing to sign up to it, to subscribe to the task it takes on: the creation of destabilizing movements in metaphysical thinking.

Is this task as important or as necessary as Derrida suggests? Not all his readers have thought so. But to dismiss Derrida's writing as wilfully *obscure* is too hasty. Understood as a rigorous unsettling of Western metaphysics, even Derrida's most bizarre strategies begin to make sense.

Let's look at two of these strategies: the use of *palaeonymics* and *neologisms.* Both exploit undecidability in the bid to undermine metaphysics.

Strategies: "Writing"

To privilege writing over speech is one thing. But it's not just a question of thinking the terms in their familiar opposition. Derrida re-conceptualizes writing as an undecidable: the play of presence/absence and radical difference, across speech as well as script. This is the play designated by Derrida's terms *the trace* and *the gram* (hence *grammatology*). And by his term *writing*.

"WRITING" BECOMES A PALAEONYMIC: OLD WORD, NEW USES. IT NO LONGER DESIGNATES SCRIPTING RATHER THAN SPEAKING BUT RATHER THE UNDECIDABLE PLAY IN BOTH. IT INHABITS SPOKEN WORDS, INSCRIBED MARKS ...

... ALL OTHER SIGNS.

How can we tell when the word is used in this sense? We can't. (Unless we add something, e.g. "writing-in-Derrida's-sense". But a supplement brings its own undecidability.) Derrida's palaeonymy is a potentiality in all uses of the word, in his own texts and others.

Derrida also coins neologisms. *Différance* is one, and it doesn't mean anything. It's a coinage which can't be exchanged...

Différance

Différance is not a French word. But it's related to some words...

the noun

la différence (with an "e") = the difference

the verb

différer = to differ, and to defer

the verb-adjective

différant = the condition of differing, or of deferring

These offer Derrida's neologism some possibilities. For instance, the verb *différer* has a play of both space and time: "things" differ spatially, "putting something off" is temporal.

And the same for the verb-adjective ("the differing shapes", "the deferring tactic").

But in French there's a semantic deficit. There's no noun-verb. We'd expect one – a word which lets us name the *activity* of "putting off", or of differing with someone or something. If *différance* were a French word, it might be that noun-verb. But it isn't. Not being that, it can supply the semantic loss *and* cover all other absences and occlusions of meaning across these related nouns, verbs, etc.

The Four Fields of Différance

With this impossible possibility (différance is [not] a French word), Derrida inserts différance into four fields of concepts and words.

1 **Insertion between speech and writing:** Différance is pronounced the same as *différence*. If spoken, différance cannot be heard. But différance can be *read.* It privileges writing, while inhabiting speech as a possibility.

2 **Insertion between nouns and verbs:** Différance is neither noun nor verb. It plays *between* "thing" and "doing", between entity and action:- a foundational opposition of philosophy.

3 **Insertion between the sensible and the intelligible:** Différance plays across both sides of the Saussurian sign (signifier and signified).

Let's look more closely at the play of the **sensible** and the **intelligible**.

– Différance exceeds *the sensible* because the sensible needs gaps of time or space which are never fully apprehensible:- in speech, pauses and delays between sounds; and in script, non-phonetic signs, spacings on the page, little marks of punctuation, etc. We can see that two graphic marks differ, but we cannot see *the difference.* Différance encompasses this.

– Différance exceeds *the intelligible*, because the sensible inhabits the intelligible. As we see from the usual words for conceptualization. Derrida's examples:- Greek *theorein* (theory) also means "to look at" or "to see"; French *entendement* (understanding) is the noun form of *entendre,* "to hear".

And finally...

4 **Insertion between words and concepts:**
Différance is neither a word (in French) nor a concept (a signified). It doesn't exist; it's not a present-being, a "thing" with essence and existence. It refuses the question, "What is différance?". Better to write: différance ⌧ Derrida crosses out the verb of being, putting it under erasure ("*sous rature*": borrowed from Heidegger). Both there and not there, cancelled but not ejected, present and absent.

Différance doesn't follow the model of the standard philosophical neologism:- a (new) word for a (new) concept. Instead, it sets in play a movement of undecidability.

Différance is actively disruptive. Language, thought and meaning aren't to be allowed the comfort of their daily routines. If that leaves philosophical language ruined, sick with its own instabilities, what about ordinary language and everyday communication? Can we rely on grounded decidability in the supermarket, the office and the lecture hall?

IT'S NOT IN THE DICTIONARY!

*MY AIM IS NOT TO JUSTIFY THE INVENTION OF THIS WORD BUT TO INTENSIFY ITS **PLAY**. EVERYTHING IS **STRATEGIC**, AND **ADVENTUROUS**. FOR THESE REASONS, THERE IS NOWHERE TO BEGIN.*

DISORDER IN COMMUNICATION

Ordinary Language

To many of his critics, Derrida simply overlooks the fact of successful communication. Ordinary language works. Therefore it's always possible – in principle, and barring accidents – to be clear, say what we mean, and to know what someone is thinking.

1971: the **Sociétés de Philosophie de Langue Française** organize a colloquium. The topic: communication. Derrida delivers a lecture, "Signature, event, context" in spoken words.

He sets up a question...

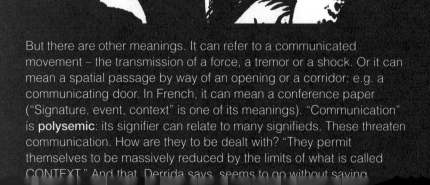

CAN THE WORD "COMMUNICATION" COMMUNICATE?

PERHAPS, SINCE IT HAS A STANDARD AND ACCEPTED MEANING. COMMUNICATION IN LANGUAGE OR DISCOURSE IMPLIES A TRANSMISSION FROM ONE PERSON TO ANOTHER OF A MEANING OR A CONCEPT. IT'S A SIGNIFIED "IN TRANSIT" AND I TAKE ISSUE WITH THAT...

But there are other meanings. It can refer to a communicated movement – the transmission of a force, a tremor or a shock. Or it can mean a spatial passage by way of an opening or a corridor: e.g. a communicating door. In French, it can mean a conference paper ("Signature, event, context" is one of its meanings). "Communication" is **polysemic**: its signifier can relate to many signifieds. These threaten communication. How are they to be dealt with? "They permit themselves to be massively reduced by the limits of what is called CONTEXT." And that, Derrida says, seems to go without saying.

The Assurance of Context

"Signature, event, context" begins with context. *How* can a context assure "correct" meanings?

Derrida's lecture had a context – a convention of French-speaking philosophers. Its communications are governed by consensus:

1. There will be linguistic communication.

2. It will be oral.

3. It will obey norms of intelligibility.

4. Agreement could in principle be established. And all this communication will be about language – not shocks and tremors, passageways, conduits, alleys, entrances, exits or conference papers. Nobody will write or mime or photograph; and the topic is not geological, etc. There will be proper communication about proper "communication". And that goes without saying.

Can these proper communications be guaranteed by context, so nobody is in any doubt? Ultimately, can *context* master the play of différance and provide meaning with a safe haven from undecidability?

Audience of French-speaking philosophers

Convention in Montreal

1971

I'M SPEAKING IN CONTEXT

Events

J. L. Austin (1911-60), Oxford "ordinary language" philosopher, believed there was a "safe context" for what he called *performative* utterances. He defined performatives in an opposition:

PERFORMATIVE utterances are speech acts which perform an action. To say "I name this ship the *Argosy*" enacts the naming: it *is* the naming, not a statement *about* the naming. Likewise with other performatives, such as those of marriage ceremonies.

CONSTATIVE utterances are assertions or statements of fact. "The cat sat on the mat" or "The practice of advanced capitalism is intimately linked with the practice of masculinism."

*ALL **PERFORMATIVES** "DO THINGS WITH WORDS", WHETHER MARRYING, PERSUADING, PROMISING, CLAIMING, INSISTING, BAPTIZING, COMPLAINING, BURYING, BETTING, GIFTING, OPENING, LAUNCHING...*

***CONSTATIVES** CAN BE JUDGED TRUE OR FALSE – AND THEY'RE THE PREFERRED UTTERANCES OF PHILOSOPHY AND THE HUMAN SCIENCES.*

OXFORD

Performatives aren't true or false, but they can succeed or fail. This depends on context. Austin's performatives need their correct context:

● a conventional **procedure** that everyone agrees to

● conventional and appropriate **persons**, **words**, and **circumstances**

● a conventional **effect**

And the procedure must be carried out *correctly* and *completely* by *all*. If all's well, the speech act is "felicitous" (appropriate and perhaps happy). If not, something might not be performed, or it might be the wrong thing.

The Etiolations of Language

So performatives can fail. There's worse: *etiolation*. Austin says:

"A performative utterance will be in a peculiar way hollow or void if said by an **actor** or on the stage, or if introduced in a **poem**, or spoken in **soliloquy**. Language in such circumstances is in special ways *not seriously* used, but used in ways *parasitic* upon its normal use – ways that fall under the doctrine of the *etiolations* of language."

ETIOLATION MEANS MAKING PALE, COLOURLESS, PALLID OR SICKLY-LOOKING. AUSTIN HAS NO CHOICE...

"All this we are excluding from consideration. Our performatives are to be understood as issued in ordinary circumstances. I must not be joking."

The fictional, theatrical and poetic – joking and non-seriousness. All this is *blanched* language, a pale imitation of its serious original. It is merely QUOTATIONAL, it simply REPEATS and RE-USES. Its performatives (and much else) are parasitical on the body of proper language.

Why does Austin exclude these? Because they are never *intended* to succeed.

Austin adopts the classic metaphysical procedure:-

1 There is SERIOUS language: it needs the presence of the speaker's intention. A performative needs its context, correct to the last detail; and its last detail is its centre, its grounding – *presence.* The speaker has to have a genuine, sincere, present *intention.* Or the speech act will lose its proper colour.

2 There is NON-SERIOUS language: it quotes, repeats, re-uses the serious original.

*AUSTIN CONJURES A KIND OF AGONY OF LANGUAGE THAT MUST BE KEPT FIRMLY AT A DISTANCE, OR FROM WHICH ONE MUST RESOLUTELY TURN AWAY. HIS ARGUMENT SUGGESTS A **RISK** SURROUNDING LANGUAGE LIKE A DITCH, INTO WHICH IT MIGHT FALL; A PLACE OF EXTERNAL PERDITION INTO WHICH LANGUAGE MIGHT NEVER VENTURE, THAT IT MIGHT AVOID BY REMAINING AT HOME.*

The ditch? **Writing ...**

The Writing Lesson: Iterability

Derrida views language differently. What Austin expels as aberrant, Derrida takes as the standard case. And this is found in writing. We've seen this already ...

> WRITING OPERATES ON **ABSENCES**. IT CAN BE CUT FREE FROM ITS SENDER AND ITS ADDRESSEE. IN THEIR ABSENCE A THIRD PARTY CAN DECIPHER IT, IDENTIFY ITS MARKS, AND USE IT.

* *iter*, "once again", from *itara*, Sanskrit "other".

Writing must therefore be ITERABLE* – *repeatable*, but in the sense of repeatable-with-*difference*. We can repeat marks we can identify; and to identify marks, we have to be able to repeat them. We could not identify or *read* a writing we could not repeat. It would not be legible.

Iterability undermines "context" as a final governor of meanings. Repeatability implies repetition *elsewhere* ...

Citations and Grafts

Iterability has many implications. CITATION is always possible. We can always lift out a sequence of words from a written tract. We can make an extract, and it can still function meaningfully. GRAFTING is equally possible. We can insert the stolen sequence (whose property was it?) into other chains of writing. As Derrida writes: "No context can enclose it." Hence writing is writing always with stolen words. Not to mention all of its quotations, plagiarisms, imitations, pastiches, etc.

> *THIS ISN'T CONFINED TO SCRIPT. ITERABILITY, CITATION AND GRAFTING ARE FOUND IN* **ALL** *SIGNS, AND IN MY SENSE, THIS MAKES THEM ALL WRITING.*

For instance, speech is iterable, citable and graftable. It's possible to say:

> She began the speech, My husband and I...

It's possible to cite oneself; and to make multiple embedded grafts. To say:

> Last week I said: She began the speech, My husband and I...

Speech, like writing, can be cut from its context, and from all the presences of its moments of utterance.

"What would a sign be that one could not cite? And whose *origin* could not be lost on the way?"

The Law of Possible Failure

Derrida confronts us with a paradox. Repeatability is the *risk* of language, its ditch and its disablement. It can derail communication.

But repeatability is also its condition of possibility. Without it, there could be no recognizable signs. Without the **possibility** of a quotational version, we can't have the "true", "real" one.

Communication can be derailed by iterability, and it carries its derailer inside itself.

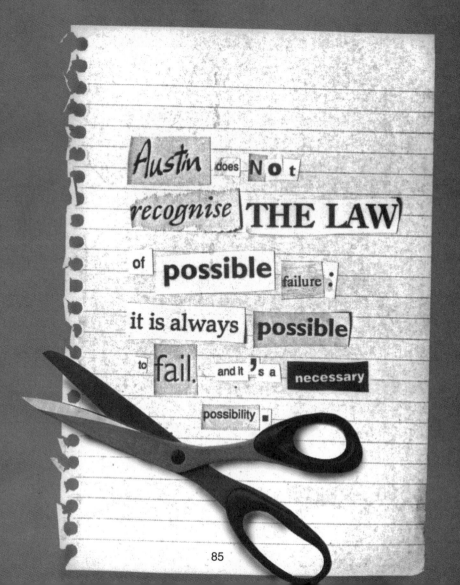

Austin does Not recognise THE LAW of possible failure: it is always possible to fail, and it's a necessary possibility.

Communication?

Derrida does *not* conclude that performatives and ordinary language lack effects; nor that the *effects* of speaking are merely the same as those of scripting. It's simply that their effects *do not exclude* what is usually opposed to them: iterability, citation, and grafting. These cannot be expelled from language. They are its necessary condition.

Does this eradicate CONTEXT? For Derrida, no. There are contexts, but they have no centre and can never entirely govern meanings.

Does it eradicate INTENTIONS? Again, no. Iterability, citationality and grafting ensure that a force of intention *will never be completely present* in an utterance or its content. And it's never completely absent.

> INTENTION DOES NOT DISAPPEAR: IT WILL HAVE ITS PLACE, BUT FROM THIS PLACE IT WILL NO LONGER BE ABLE TO GOVERN THE ENTIRE SCENE AND THE ENTIRE SYSTEM OF UTTERANCES.

Communication? It is perhaps possible, if by communication we mean transactions which presuppose repetition-with-difference, quotation and re-insertions, without boundaries. And that could lead to some rethinking of everyday life.

INTENTION DOES NOT DISAPPEAR!

SAYS EGGHEAD JACQUES

Trendy French boffin Jacques Derrida reckons that even though you think you know what you're saying, there's nothing to stop people from quoting your words out of context.

Pull the other one ' Just tell that to

Signatures and Paraphs

There are signatures, every day. To Austin they are performative acts in writing. They follow his model. Legal signatures especially need an intending source *present* to the inscription in its moment of production. Signatures gain their power from this assumption ...

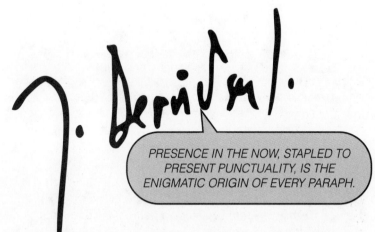

PRESENCE IN THE NOW, STAPLED TO PRESENT PUNCTUALITY, IS THE ENIGMATIC ORIGIN OF EVERY PARAPH.

Paraph: flourish, embroidered underlining, "knot"; also, to sign with initials only; to sign with a flourish, with name or without. (O.E.D.) The paraph is a supplement.

But Derrida sees the signature as writing. To function, it must be iterable: repeatable, imitable. It must be detachable from the signatory and the signatory's intentions. There is no *need* for a particular intention at the point of signing.

Therefore signatures can be *counterfeited*, maybe fraudulently. This is necessary. To repeat "one's own" signature (as if we could possess the marks) is always to counterfeit, to imitate. How else could we write the marks, would we know which marks to inscribe?

All of which makes the signature dubious. It's always double, because always inhabited by the threat and the necessity of its repeatability. It could never give assurance if it could not be doubted.

The signature is doubtful. Does this destroy it? There are signatures, every day...

> ITERABILITY IS THE CONDITION OF POSSIBILITY OF THE SIGNATURE, BUT IT IS **ALSO THE CONDITION OF ITS IMPOSSIBILITY**, OF THE IMPOSSIBILITY OF ITS RIGOROUS PURITY. ITS DETACHABILITY CORRUPTS ITS IDENTITY AND ITS SINGULARITY, DIVIDES ITS SEAL.

Derrida's "Signature, event, context" ends with Derrida's signature. He signs with an im/pure signature, a paraph and a re-mark.

> Writing therefore, if there is any, perhaps communicates, but does not exist, surely. Or barely, hereby, in the form of the most improbable signature.

> *J. Derrida.*

> (*Remark:* the – written – text of this – oral – communication was to have been addressed to the *Association of French-Speaking Societies of Philosophy* before the meeting. Such a missive therefore had to be signed. Which I did, and counterfeit here. Where? There. J.D.)

What's important in this argument about communication and signatures?

Derrida has argued that communication is always subject to iterability, citation and grafting. If so, it can't be taken as a guaranteed, masterable passage of meanings. Language, Derrida says, is a "non-masterable dissemination".

If that's the case, we lose absolute assurance that we can "say what we mean" or "know what someone is thinking".

I HAVE HERE A PIECE OF PAPER SIGNED BY HERR HITLER AND MYSELF ...

We can't even be sure who is speaking or writing: the identity of the author or signatory who appears to have produced the discourse, who's signed for it, and who's supposed to be – in the logocentric view – the origin or centre of the discourse.

Derrida derails communication, introducing disorder into its foundational concepts.

We've been following the two strands of Derrida's proposed "matrix" of inquiry – **undecidability**, with its disruption of foundational oppositions, and the **introduction of disorder into communication**.

It leads to thinking and writing of an unfamiliar kind: undoing, undermining, destabilizing, decomposing, desedimenting ...

• Derrida's texts aren't located "outside" the texts they examine, in a position of attempted mastery or privileged authority. He doesn't simply reject or oppose them. It's more a strategy of inhabiting them, making a destabilizing passage through them, undoing their presuppositions and desedimenting them: stirring up their underlying levels.

• Derrida's texts need their "host" texts. In a sense, they're parasitical. The undecidables need the oppositions they disrupt. Yet the "host" texts already contain the elements which will undo them – Plato has his *pharmakon*, Austin his iterating etiolations – even if these are usually overlooked, denied, called to order, or given an eviction notice.

• Undecidability and derailments of communication are always and already at work, in all discourse – in law, politics, education, the military, medicine, etc, as well as in philosophy and theory.

Derrida's task has been to intensify their disruptive play. His strategies and tactics have been given a name: DECONSTRUCTION. But in many ways, Derrida's writing has scarcely needed it ...

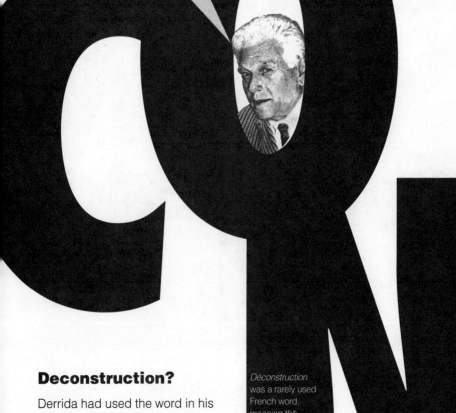

DECONSTRUCTION IS A WORD WHOSE FORTUNES HAVE DISAGREEABLY SURPRISED ME. I LITTLE THOUGHT IT WOULD BE CREDITED WITH SUCH A CENTRAL ROLE – IT'S BEEN OF SERVICE IN A CERTAIN SITUATION, BUT IT'S NEVER APPEARED SATISFACTORY TO ME. IT'S NOT A GOOD WORD, AND NOT ELEGANT.

Deconstruction?

Derrida had used the word in his early writings. It adapted and translated the German *Destruktion* or *Abbau*, terms Heidegger had used in his re-examination of metaphysics. For Derrida, the French word *destruction* was too negative and one-sided. It suggested antagonistic demolition or eradication. In Derrida's uses, *déconstruction* designated a double movement: both disordering, or disarrangement, and also re-arranging.

Déconstruction was a rarely used French word, meaning the grammatical re-arrangement of words in a sentence; or as a verb, *déconstruire*, to dis-assemble a machine, as for transport.

Deconstruction *is* ... ?

It's been a problematic word. In a letter to Toshiko Izutsu*, Japanese Islamologist, Derrida asks: can it be defined? Can it be translated, for instance into Japanese?

[* *Letter to a Japanese Friend*, 1983]

First: any terms used to translate it – or to define it, by offering it definitive meanings or concepts – are themselves open to deconstructive operations.

Secondly, is there "something" to be defined or translated? Derrida has resisted the suggestion that there is a concept of deconstruction, simply present to the word, outside of the word's inscription in sentences and phrases determined by the undecidables. There's no such concept simply to *pass over* into other words, other languages.

In Derrida's view this is a problem for translation in general. Translators have to say, and not say, what someone has said.

It's Not What You Think?

Definitions and translations are always open to the classic metaphysical procedures, especially their ontological move: to determine being as presence. Deconstruction, Derrida suggests, might be better described as *a suspicion against thinking "what is the essence of?"*.

> *ALL SENTENCES OF THE TYPE "DECONSTRUCTION IS X" OR "DECONSTRUCTION IS NOT X" **A PRIORI** MISS THE POINT, WHICH IS TO SAY THAT THEY ARE AT LEAST FALSE. ONE OF THE PRINCIPAL THINGS IN DECONSTRUCTION IS THE DELIMITING OF ONTOLOGY AND ABOVE ALL OF THE THIRD PERSON PRESENT INDICATIVE: **S** IS **P**.*

Geoff Bennington offers an aphorism: *"Deconstruction is not what you think. If what you think is a concept, present to mind. But that you think might already be Deconstruction."*

– ism?

To name deconstruction is to call it to order, to harness it to familiar, stable, logocentric notions of what thinking should be. Surely, ultimately, deconstruction must be a mode of **analysis** or **critique**; or a **method** or a **project**. Derrida has resisted this.

It leads to "deconstructionism"...

Analysis seeks to distinguish simple, undivided elements which can then be treated as originary and explanatory. In its operations on Western metaphysics, deconstruction resists the move towards simple elements or origins.

Critique in the usual sense implies a stance outside its object. Deconstruction insists on movements across and between the metaphysical opposites, inside/outside.

Method, in Derrida's view, operates by selecting out certain terms of a discourse and using them to name something *technical* or *procedural*. He's identified this especially in deconstruction in the United States, e.g. in aspects of the literary criticism known as Yale Deconstruction.

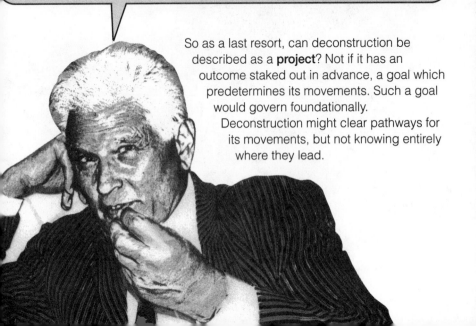

THIS LEADS TO DOMESTICATIONS, REAPPROPRIATIONS BY ACADEMIC INSTITUTIONS.

So as a last resort, can deconstruction be described as a **project**? Not if it has an outcome staked out in advance, a goal which predetermines its movements. Such a goal would govern foundationally.
Deconstruction might clear pathways for its movements, but not knowing entirely where they lead.

Doesn't this place deconstruction, and its adherents, in an impossible position, a "non-place" of contemporary thought?

In 1967, Derrida concluded his essay "Structure, Sign and Play" by posing a question between two types of thinking. One dreams of deciphering a truth or origin which escapes play; the other turns away from the origin, and affirms play.

It's a question maybe of choice – or in Derrida's view, of the historical necessity of "relinquishing the dream of full presence": the reassuring foundation, the origin and the end of play.

IT'S A QUESTION WHOSE **CONCEPTION, FORMATION, GESTATION** AND **LABOUR** WE ARE ONLY CATCHING A GLIMPSE OF TODAY. SOME WILL TURN THEIR EYES AWAY WHEN FACED BY THE AS-YET UNNAMEABLE WHICH IS **PROCLAIMING** ITSELF, AND WHICH CAN DO SO – AS IS NECESSARY WHEN A BIRTH IS IN THE OFFING – ONLY UNDER THE SPECIES OF THE NONSPECIES, IN THE FORMLESS, MUTE, INFANT AND TERRIFYING FORM OF MONSTROSITY.

Unformed, monstrous, and perhaps unidentifiable, deconstruction has moved virally through fields beyond philosophy and theory. Derrida has advanced its progress in architecture, art, politics and law. And especially, in literature...

WRITING AND LITERATURE

By the 1950s, philosophy and literature in France had new points of contact. The Surrealist poets of the 1930s had addressed philosophical issues. The novels, plays and poetry of **Albert Camus** (1913-60), **Jean-Paul Sartre** (1905-80) and others explored Existentialist themes. And **Paul Valéry** (1871-1945), Mallarméan poet and critic, saw philosophy as a practice of writing and therefore as a sub-category of literature. Derrida took a cue from Valéry. It is necessary to study philosophical texts like literary texts. We need to pay attention to their styles, forms, figures of speech – even their titles, layouts, and typography.

But traditionally, the philosophical search for *truth* has claimed precedence over literature's concern with *style*.

Literary Texts, Philosophical Texts

Unlike Valéry, Derrida had little interest in simply OVERTURNING the hierarchical claims of philosophy over literature. He looked for ways of destabilizing or DISPLACING the boundaries between them, putting the categories themselves into question.

THERE'S NO ASSURED ESSENCE OF "LITERATURE" OR "PHILOSOPHY". THEY'RE UNSTABLE CATEGORIES WITH NO GUARANTEES. IF THEY SEEM SECURE AND NATURAL, IT'S BECAUSE THEY'RE GOVERNED BY A POWERFUL CONSENSUS, PREMISED ON FOUNDATIONAL THINKING.

LITERATURE

Their boundaries can never be entirely certain. Texts have *traits*, characteristics which they share with other texts. And a literary text can share some of its traits with philosophical, legal or political texts, etc.

Derrida exploits this. If the categories and boundaries are disturbed, the hierarchy too might begin to lose its grip.

Contamination

So Derrida opens literature and philosophy to a mutual CONTAMINATION. It's a deconstructive strategy. Certain characteristics of philosophy and literature might remain, but they won't be allowed an assured, overarching mastery of what is written and how it is read.

WHAT INTERESTS ME IS NOT STRICTLY CALLED EITHER PHILOSOPHY OR LITERATURE. I DREAM OF A WRITING THAT WOULD BE NEITHER, WHILE STILL KEEPING – I'VE NO DESIRE TO ABANDON THIS – THE **MEMORY** OF LITERATURE AND PHILOSOPHY.

What can philosophy gain from its own contamination? Studying literature can reveal something about philosophy's *limits of interpretation*. That's Derrida's main interest.

He's pursued it in two ways. He's written *about* literary texts, though not producing standard literary criticism. But also, he's borrowed devices and strategies from literary writing, and put them to use in his destabilization of metaphysics.

Writing at the Limits

Searching out texts that have "made the limits of our language tremble", Derrida has turned to avant-garde literature, to the modernist or postmodern writings of Mallarmé, Kafka, Joyce, Ponge, Blanchot and others.

In 1974 he wrote an essay, "Mallarmé", for the series *Tableau de la littérature française.* It's one of Derrida's many engagements with texts by **Stéphane Mallarmé** (1842-98), poet and prose writer, modernist and Symbolist.

Mallarmé's writing has usually been seen as a poetic exploitation of **semantic richness** – the potential of language for multiple meanings, references and allusions. Derrida reads it instead as a **decomposition of linguistic elements**, and especially of the word..

Mallarmé's *Or* (Gold) plays on *"or"* as two letters, a syllable and a word. It's all three.

Mallarmé has *words* of "gold"...
d'éclats d'or [gleams of gold]
dorure [gilding]

... but he also exploits *"or"* as *letters* inside words:
majORe [increase]
trésOR [treasure]
dehORs [outside]
hORizon [horizon]
fantasmagORiques [phantasmagorical]

Even as a word, *"or"* isn't stable. It's a **noun** ("gold"), but also an **adjective** ("golden") and a **conjunction** ("now"):- "*une éclipse, **or**, telle est l'heure*" ("an eclipse, *now*, such is the hour").

For Mallarmé the order of words is important. He often places *"or"* after *"son"* ("his" or "its", a possessive adjective; but also the noun "sound"):-

"*son or*" ("his gold" or "golden sound"). Also, in French this *sounds* like "*sonore*" (= "sonorous", an adjective).

He makes "*son*" hesitate between adjective and noun.

Especially, "*le son or*" can mean either "the golden sound" or "the sound *or*" – just the sound of the syllable, the oratorical material.

And Mallarmé, author of *Les Mots Anglais*, knew that "*or*" can be a syllable, or a word, or letters, in English or French.

> THERE'S NO NOUN, NO THING WHICH IS SIMPLY NAMED – IT'S ALSO A CONJUNCTION, AN ADJECTIVE, ETC.
>
> ## NO MORE WORD:
>
> ONE SYLLABLE CAN SCATTER THE WORD.

semantic indecision. And it arises from the unsettling *placing* of letters, sounds, words – from *syntax* (the location of linguistic elements) not semantics (meanings). In fact, it upsets, derails, meanings. Derrida's interest is not the supposed rich content, the semantic luxuriousness, but the dislocation of content by strategic syntaxing.

This might work in philosophy too. Mallarméan syntaxing resists the assured content of crucial, foundational philosophical words like "truth", "being" or "origin". So Derrida decomposes words. Différance, neither noun nor verb (no word, no concept), undermines the stable order of meaning demanded by logocentric texts.

BEING
TRUTH
ORIGIN

Reading Mallarmé

What has this to do with "Stéphane Mallarmé"? Derrida turns
aside the usual questions of literary criticism. AUTHORSHIP, for
instance. Can the author be *present* to the text, governing its
meanings? Must we study authors? At the end of "Mallarmé",
Derrida recites the law.

*ONE SHOULD HAVE SPOKEN OF STÉPHANE MALLARMÉ, OF HIS THOUGHT,
OF HIS UNCONSCIOUS AND HIS THEMES, OF WHAT HE SEEMED TO WANT TO
SAY. ONE SHOULD HAVE SPOKEN OF HIS INFLUENCES; OF HIS **LIFE**, FIRST OF
ALL – OF HIS BEREAVEMENTS AND HIS DEPRESSIONS, OF HIS TEACHING, OF
HIS TRAVELS, OF HIS FAMILY AND FRIENDS, OF THE LITERARY SALONS, ETC.
UNTIL THE FINAL SPASM OF THE GLOTTIS.*

Author's intentions, thoughts, milieux? These are common critical
categories. In Derrida's view, none of them offers an assured
foundation for interpretation. And they're premised on
metaphysical oppositions. They presuppose possibilities of
decision with no pertinence to the strategies of Mallarmé's texts.

Ulysses Gramophone

In 1984, Derrida was invited to open the 9th International James Joyce Symposium in Frankfurt. What could he say to these experts in Joyce, these guardians perhaps of *decision* in literature?

As literary criticism, "Ulysses Gramophone" is unusual. It inhabits and imitates the mock epic novel *Ulysses* (1922), Joyce's account of 16 June 1904 in Dublin, a day unmarked by any important event. Derrida's text has accounts of its own textual composition, of how it received its title, of Derrida searching for a postcard of lakes in Tokyo, of "the battle of Tokio" in *Ulysses,* etc. Like *Ulysses,* it has circuitous journeys – Oxford, Ohio, Tokyo, Paris – and inserts a figure of its author: Elijah enters, as a polymathic telematic switchboard operator, and figure of unpredictability. (Derrida has the Hebrew name Elijah, French *Elie.*) It's a text unmarked by any extraordinary event ...

"yes"

in Joyce's Ulysses

Like *Ulysses,* "Ulysses Gramophone" repeats, cites, grafts, and sometimes syntactically decomposes. These are its ordinary everyday events. Derrida's concern is to keep them in play, not fixed down by standard scholarly procedures.

How does he do this? He examines, for instance, the word "yes", much repeated in *Ulysses.* How can it be interpreted? What are its *limits* of interpretation? His own text demonstrates the difficulties.

"Oui, oui, vous m'entendez bien, ce sont des mots français."

They can't be translated entirely. But partly in English:

"Oui, Oui, you are receiving me well, these are French words."

It's a sentence that derails translation. ("Yes, yes, these are *not* French words"?) Derrida, reading between French and English versions of *Ulysses*, wants to keep open the idea of a translation as a new text, not as a copy which simply delivers the meanings of an original.

And we have another problem: citation. Does Derrida's second "yes" *quote* his first "yes" (or some other "yes")? We can't be sure, because he might be *using* the second '"yes", for emphasis maybe, or to affirm the first "yes" – to say yes to "yes". Between quotation and use, it's undecidable.

So we were not receiving Derrida very well at all, not able to know "what he wanted to say". Can we receive, loud and clear, *yeses* from Joyce?

Other Yeses

Perhaps some standard scholarly procedures might help. Derrida adopts some, perhaps ironically.

First, find all the yeses. Derrida gets about 222. It seems a close reading. But perhaps a computer could help.

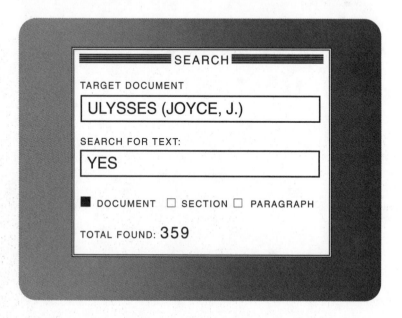

A computer *has* been used, and it came up with 359. But how could the limits of this task ever be finally established? How could the programmers decide what to exclude? The Ayes? The other affirmatives ("he nodded")? The non-English yeses, the *si*'s and the *oui*'s?

And the yeses would need organizing into interpretative categories. Derrida gets as far, perhaps, as ten. Yeses can be read as question forms, signs of obedience or servility (yes, sir), agreements to facts, yeses of desire, of absent-minded politeness, etc. *But such a list could never be closed.*

And are these yeses decidably *uses* or *quotations*?

Undecidability eludes the contemporary machineries of interpretation, even that of the Joyce industry.

In the Name of Joyce

The computer is derailed. And the Joyce experts?

When you call on the external competence of philosophers, psychoanalysts, linguists, etc, is it not both to humiliate them, and because you expect from them news - good news come at last to deliver you from the hypermnesic interiority in which you go round in circles like hallucinators in a nightmare?

We should get rid of a double illusion and a double intimidation. (1) No truth can come from outside the Joycean community, and without the experience, the cunning, and the knowledge amassed by trained readers. But (2) also, there's no model for "Joycean" competence, no closure possible for it. There is no absolute criterion for measuring the relevance of a discourse on the subject of a text signed by "Joyce".

The Tasks of Criticism

Derrida's procedures have been unusual.

- He unsettles the usual relations between the literary work and the critical text. His writing doesn't just *respond* to *Ulysses*, it is partly *like* it. It's a creative work, sharing in Joyce's project, borrowing its literary devices. And that's been an attractive idea to many literary critics.

- Derrida searches out the limits of interpretation – the points where standard critical procedures break down, where assured interpretation fails. Neither AUTHORSHIP studies nor CLOSE ANALYTICAL READINGS can escape these points of failure.

- And Derrida takes the literary establishment to task for assuming that it can mark out the space of its own expertise, containing itself safely within its own boundaries and mastering whatever is inside them – e.g. texts signed by the name "Joyce".

Opening Up the Text

What's left of "foundations" for literary criticism? Perhaps THE TEXT. Surely we can be sure that we have texts.

But what is a text? If we're to be certain, a text will need some decidable characteristics. Preferably it will have:–

Some **edges** or **boundaries**, marking out its inside from its outside, so that it can be treated as a unified "body", with limits. We must know where to stop, where to start.

It should belong to a recognizable **genre**, assuring us what *type* of text it is: novel, essay, play, poem, etc.

A **title**, properly one that names it.

An **author**, or signatories of some kind.

Derrida opens these up and destabilizes them – not just by writing *about* them, but by making texts in which they perform differently. *Glas* is perhaps his best-known example...

Glas

Glas (1974) is a very unorthodox text. It has two vertical columns, disrupted by quotational inserts from different authors in different typographical styles, formats and languages. It's perhaps a radical collage.

Derrida's left hand column concerns one of philosophy's "great names"...	In the right hand column, Derrida's account of another writer...

Georg Wilhelm Friedrich HEGEL (1770-1831): German idealist philosopher, Professor at the Universities of Jena, Heidelberg, Berlin, author of the *Phenomenology of Spirit*, the *Logic* and the *Philosophy of Right*; proponent of world history as the history of the *Geist* (spirit, or *logos*) in its progress towards self-conscious awareness, an "uplifting" dialectical progress towards absolute knowledge...

Jean GENET (1910-86): illegitimately-born French writer, thief, recidivist, life prisoner of the French government under the law of the *relège*; Marseilles rent-boy who "masculinized" his "feminine" homosexuality through work (burglary); literary artist supported by Sartre and other intellectuals, author of the autobiographical *Thief's Journal*, of novels, plays and performance scenarios (*Our Lady of the Flowers, The Maids, 'Adame Miroir*, etc).

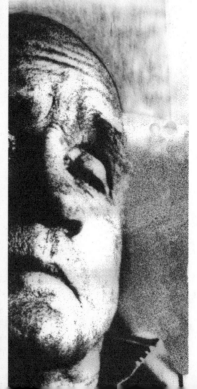

Glas opens philosophy to literature. Neither column can be read without its internal edge constantly opening on to the other. And in each column, Derrida cites and grafts from Hegel's personal letters and documents, from his philosophical texts, from Genet's journal of the thief and his prose-poetry.

circulation du jouir dans le culte. *Telos* du culte, spéculer, la jouissance de Dieu et se la faire.

en suivant la galerie phénoménologique (« Ce devenir présente (stellt... dar) un mouvement lent et une conséquence d'esprits, une galerie d'images (eine Galerie von Bildern)... »), de station en station, on revient vers l'IC et le Sa, passé le « calvaire de l'esprit absolu ». On y retrouve, tout près du « calvaire », — à inspecter des deux côtés — la « certitude de son trône » (Gewissheit seines Throns).
Il suffit en somme, à peine, d'attendre.
Tout cela aura été projeté, mis en pièces, clos, cloué, tombé, relevé, répété, aux alentours de Pâques.
Le cercle de la galerie phénoménologique se reproduit et s'encercle dans la grande logique et dans l'Encyclopédie. Quelle est la différence entre deux éditions du même cercle? Hegel qui vient d'apprendre « la vente rapide de la deuxième édition » de l'Encyclopédie, confie à Winter, en 1827, ses inquiétudes. Il lui demande de se porter « garant du paiement ponctuel des honoraires ». « Pour le nombre de feuilles primitif (18) dans la première édition, nous avons fixé les deux tiers de l'honoraire, se montant à 25 florins; pour le nombre de feuilles postérieur, nous sommes revenus à cet honoraire, et pour les 18 autres feuilles de la deuxième édition, nous nous sommes contentés de 22 florins par feuille; en concluant cet accord, je me suis réservé le droit de réclamer des honoraires pour ce qui serait ajouté dans une nouvelle édition. [...] Ce nombre de feuilles s'accroîtra-t-il dans la nouvelle édition, et de combien? Je ne puis encore en avoir aucune idée, étant donné que le travail m'a surpris à l'improviste et que je n'ai encore pu parcourir l'ouvrage de ce point de vue; mais d'une façon générale, je prévois que je n'apporterai pas de modification ou d'addition importante. — Le tirage reste fixé comme auparavant à 1 000 exemplaires, avec 18 exemplaires d'auteur, 12 sur vélin et 6 sur papier à écrire.
« Du fait que j'ai reçu si tard l'annonce du besoin d'une nouvelle édition (la lettre de M. Oswald est datée du 13 juillet), il résulte que l'envoi du manuscrit ne pourra avoir lieu que tard — plus tard sans doute que vous ne le souhaitez; avec mes travaux, qui depuis se sont accumulés, je ne puis encore rien dire de précis sur la date; mais je ferai mon possible pour que l'édition puisse paraître à Pâques. »

gymnastique.

Nous sommes dans le cercle dionysiaque. Le troisième moment de l'art abstrait, la religion qui s'y inscrit, c'est déjà la phase la plus abstraite du moment ultérieur, l'œuvre d'art vivante. A travers son syllogisme, un procès de langage s'affaire encore à la relève du reste.
Le premier moment unilatéral, c'est le délire bachique, le *Taumel*, l'ivresse débordante au cours de laquelle le dieu se rend présent. L'essence lumineuse ascendante se dévoile comme ce qu'elle est. La jouissance est le mystère de cette révélation. Car le mystique ne réside pas dans la dissimulation d'un secret (Geheimnis) ou d'un insu. Mais ce qui se dénude ici appartient encore à l'esprit immédiat, à l'esprit-nature. Le mystère du pain et du vin *n'est pas encore ce qu'il est, déjà,* celui de la chair et du sang. Dionysos doit donc passer dans son contraire, s'apaiser pour exister, ne pas se laisser boire et consommer par la « horde des femmes exaltées ».
Il fait alors de la

So is *Glas* properly a text?

Glas has edges, authors, a title, etc. But not of a stable kind.

An author?
Glas has *multiple* signatories and their authority is placed in doubt. (Signatures are always "divided", Derrida says.) Even the names are destabilized. Hegel rhymes *aigle* (eagle), and Genet, *genêt* (broom-flower). Derrida plays on these, taking names as *words,* subject to decomposition, rather than simple designators of people.

114

A title?
Glas in French means "knell", the solemn toll of a bell. And it's close to other words, like *glace* (ice; mirror or window glass). It's more a word than a name for a philosophical or critical text. *Glas* strikes as an impropriety, an abuse in naming.

Edges and boundaries?
Glas has edges, but so many they *spoil* the text – they divide it up inside itself. There's no wholeness or unity, no proper body of the text. And its fragments offer multiple beginnings and endings.

As for **genre**, should we look to literature (scenario, prose-poem, collage) or philosophy (essay, exegesis, dialogue, critique, commentary, colloquy)? Or could we, like Derrida, recognize that it's impossible *not to mix* genres?

Glas is almost a text, and a little more than one.

Philosophy, Literary Art

Some critics have read *Glas* as an art work, bracketing out its philosophical concerns.

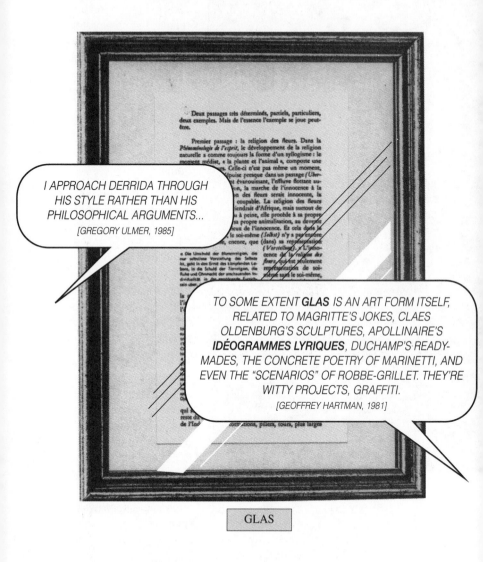

I APPROACH DERRIDA THROUGH HIS STYLE RATHER THAN HIS PHILOSOPHICAL ARGUMENTS...
[GREGORY ULMER, 1985]

TO SOME EXTENT **GLAS** IS AN ART FORM ITSELF, RELATED TO MAGRITTE'S JOKES, CLAES OLDENBURG'S SCULPTURES, APOLLINAIRE'S **IDÉOGRAMMES LYRIQUES**, DUCHAMP'S READY-MADES, THE CONCRETE POETRY OF MARINETTI, AND EVEN THE "SCENARIOS" OF ROBBE-GRILLET. THEY'RE WITTY PROJECTS, GRAFFITI.
[GEOFFREY HARTMAN, 1981]

GLAS

But there might be philosophical reasons to destabilize the text, to play with authorship, boundaries, etc. Derrida is offering a critique of Hegel's arguments for *paternal authority*, for the *family*, for the *Holy Family* and the *State* in the regulation of truth and its guaranteed passage through authorized channels.

So there's much at stake in the encounter between Hegel, the philosopher of right, and Genet, the seaport rent-boy – the conduct of philosophy in its search for truth, but also governance by the state and by the laws of patriarchy.

Derrida's text turns philosophers, thieves, fathers and families into unstable figures. Their identities are no longer assured, and neither are the usual hierarchies – the sacrosanct writing of "truth", the guaranteed "transmissions" of knowledge.

In *Glas,* the texts of the philosopher have no assured resistance to those of the literary writer, the thief, or others. Once philosophy admits that it is writing, its boundaries are not secure.

ARCHITECTURE

To Derrida, movements beyond philosophy
and literature were necessary. If logocentric
thinking isn't confined to *linguistic*
phenomena, neither is deconstruction.

So Derrida and others have put
deconstruction to work in non-linguistic
fields, such as architecture and art.

*DECONSTRUCTION IS PURELY LINGUISTIC? THAT'S
A GROSS MISUNDERSTANDING, OR A POLITICAL
STRATEGY TO **LIMIT** DECONSTRUCTION.*

Deconstructive Architecture

Deconstruction in *architecture* sounds unlikely – undermining foundations, shaking entire structures? Could it be practical, beautiful, inhabitable?

In 1988 it almost became a Movement. The Museum of Modern Art (MOMA) in New York exhibited work by seven architects under the curatorial title "Deconstructivist Architecture". Ten years of marginalized debates gathered somewhere near a centre.

The architects at MOMA had different attitudes to deconstruction. They'd all been challenging architectural assumptions, but only two of them used the term "deconstruction" in something like Derrida's sense: **Peter Eisenman** (b. 1932) and **Bernard Tschumi** (b. 1943).

In 1982, Tschumi, a 39-year-old French-Swiss architect living in New York, had been chosen to design an "Urban Park for the 21st Century", at La Villette, Paris. It became a focus for debates about deconstructive architecture.

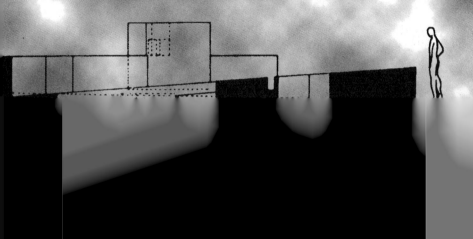

Le Parc de la Villette

The Park was an official French government project, one of François Mitterrand's *Grands Projets d'urbanisme parisien*. Like other projects of the 80s – the Bastille Opéra, Louvre Pyramid, and Grande Arche at La Défense – it was aesthetically, politically and economically controversial. The Presidential committee allocated a 125-acre site and $200m budget.

The site was a former slaughterhouse and market, Baron Haussmann's 1867 scheme for modern, "efficient" meat-processing in the north east corner of metropolitan Paris. Bordered by canals, railways and the Boulevard Macdonald, it's at the heart of a working-class area with a large immigrant population.

Largely completed by 1992, the Park is not so much a recreation of natural landscape as a 1km-long urban entertainment-leisure complex.

IT'S THE LARGEST DISCONTINUOUS BUILDING IN THE WORLD.

Deconstruction at the Park

Tschumi proposed an "architecture of disjunction". Could this be seen as deconstructive?

(1) It upsets architectural assumptions about systems.

The Park has systems: of *points, surfaces* and *lines*. But they're superimposed so that they mutually distort and sometimes clash with each other. Paths intersect buildings, ramps and steps are cut off, etc. The systems avoid synthesis. There's no single coherent *outcome*.

(2) It's a contaminated architecture.

Tschumi encouraged the architectural to collide with non-architectural ideas, elements, forms, etc, from cinema, literature and other cultural fields. "It encourages conflict over synthesis, fragmentation over unity, madness and play over careful management."

This scarcely sounds *functional*...

Functional *Folie*

Tschumi promoted a "programmatic instability", challenging the usual ideas of programmed *usefulness* in architecture. "If architecture historically has been the harmonious synthesis of COST, STRUCTURE and USE, then the Park is architecture against itself."

Tschumi provided the Park with 41 *Folies*: deformed 10m square cubes of red steel. They might be functional, but Tschumi tried to avoid specifying functions in advance. So far, the *Folies* have been cafés, video studios, a postal station and a children's playroom. There's been a folly-belvedere, and an information centre folly.

Fr. *folie* = madness, nonsense, extravagance, and small country house

If we expect a building to proclaim itself in terms of decidable functions, the *Folies* are perhaps undecidable.

"We're encouraging the combination of apparently incompatible activities (the running track passes through the piano bar inside the tropical greenhouse.)"

So the clinic contaminates the garbage dump; and the ministerial residence, the textile workers' sweatshop? It's a far-reaching notion for the politics of architecture.

Are Tschumi's tactics deconstructive in Derrida's sense? Critics have been divided. So what has Derrida said about architecture?

In the1980s he contributed essays and interviews to the debates, writing about Tschumi's Park and other aspects of deconstructive architecture...

DECONSTRUCTION OCCURS IN ARCHITECTURE WHEN YOU HAVE DECONSTRUCTED SOME ARCHITECTURAL PHILOSOPHY, SOME ARCHITECTURAL ASSUMPTIONS.

Derrida's view might be considered in two ways...

1. Challenging the authority of philosophical concepts in architecture

Architecture has relied on "essential" or "fundamental" oppositions, metaphysical in style and open to deconstructive moves ...

THEORY PRACTICE
FORM FUNCTION
INSIDE OUTSIDE
PRESENCE ABSENCE
UTILE INUTILE
AESTHETIC NON-AESTHETIC
HABITABLE UNINHABITABLE

Deconstruction might undermine architecture's philosophically-derived concepts.

If so, there's more at stake than making buildings *look* as if they're falling apart, slipping down hillsides or exploding from within. There's no visual *appearance* laid down in advance for a deconstructive building.

2. Questioning architectural thinking in philosophy

Western philosophy has often used architectonic terms – metaphors of base and superstructure, foundations and edifices, and founding moments and founding fathers. For instance, Descartes in the 17th century wrote of "the founding of a town" to describe his inauguration of a new rationalist philosophy.

Heidegger, too, used architectural terms: the edifice or grounded structure, and later, language as the house, the enclosing home or dwelling-place of Being.

LANGUAGE IS THE HOUSE OF BEING. IN ITS HOME MAN DWELLS.

Architectonic thinking is logocentric. A deconstructive architecture might resonate back into philosophy, disturbing the power of these metaphors. So can philosophy and architecture find points of close exchange?

Collaborations: Philosophy and Architecture

In 1983, Tschumi invited Derrida to collaborate with New York architect Peter Eisenman on a garden for La Villette. Derrida was working on Plato's *Timaeus,* and it entered the project. *Timaeus* is the first Greek account of the creation of the natural world by a purposeful, divine craftsman-Creator.

But Plato has a problem. He maintains that every object has both an *ideal* form – a purely intelligible, perfect and eternal model – and a changing *sensible* copy. The copy must have some *place* in which it can be created. Plato conjures one: a receptacle, or **chora**.

Timaeus is delivering the speech ...

WE MUST TRY TO DESCRIBE IN WORDS A FORM THAT IS DIFFICULT AND OBSCURE. IT IS THE RECEPTACLE AND, AS IT WERE, THE NURSE OF ALL BECOMING AND CHANGE...

WE CAN USE THE METAPHOR OF BIRTH. COMPARE THE RECEPTACLE TO THE **MOTHER**, THE IDEAL MODEL TO THE **FATHER**, AND WHAT THEY PRODUCE TO THEIR **OFFSPRING** ...

IT IS A KIND OF NEUTRAL PLASTIC MATERIAL, MALLEABLE, LIKE GOLD. THE THINGS WHICH PASS IN AND OUT OF IT ARE COPIES OF THE ETERNAL REALITIES ...

AND WE MAY NOTICE, THAT ANYTHING THAT IS TO RECEIVE IN ITSELF **EVERY** KIND OF CHARACTER MUST BE DEVOID OF **ALL** CHARACTER.

THE RECEPTACLE IS INVISIBLE AND FORMLESS, ALL-EMBRACING, POSSESSED IN A MOST PUZZLING WAY OF INTELLIGIBILITY, YET VERY HARD TO GRASP...

IT'S SOMETHING BETWEEN CONTAINER AND CONTAINED. LIKE THE SAND ON THE BEACH: IT'S NOT AN OBJECT OR A PLACE, BUT MERELY THE RECORD OF THE MOVEMENT OF WATER.

Derrida's philosophical interest is that this non-place might escape classic ontologies. It's a *spacing* rather than a place. It resists presence.

> THE **CHORA** IS A **SPACING** THAT IS THE NECESSARY CONDITION FOR EVERYTHING TO TAKE PLACE. IT CANNOT BE REPRESENTED.

Plato can describe it only by piling up elaborate metaphors. So Derrida explores the metaphors, especially those of femininity. The *chora* is matrixial, womb-like; it's the mother and the nurse. Derrida plays on the letter L, in French also *elle*.

And *chora* is a word, open to decomposition: ... choral ... vocal chords ... chorale ... the name Corelli; coral, "precious and petrified" ... choreographies ...

Could this non-space be considered architecturally? Derrida offered some possibilities: maybe an obliquely-planted, gilded metallic object; or a solid frame, hatched or grilled like a sieve or a stringed instrument; and an aerial telescope or camera filter, a photographic or radiographic machine, in rapport with the rest.

WE FINALLY FORCED JACQUES TO DRAW SOMETHING.

Choral Work

Eisenman had been working deconstructively since the late 1970s, questioning architectural oppositions: interior/exterior, structure/decoration, etc.

He came up with a polychoral design, citing three texts:-

• His own earlier housing project for Cannaregio, Venice.

• Derrida's text on the *chora,* and his drawing.

• Tschumi's plan for the Park, quoted in miniature.

"Choral Work" has an inclined steel ground plane with acid-etched lines tracing Tschumi's systems.

Eisenman deployed his "quarrying" strategy: expose the foundations of a site, its history, and include them in the work. If they're not there, build them. So "Choral Work" includes constructed fragments of the old Paris city walls, in white marble; and underground, the 1867 abattoirs.

There are elevated "El [*elle*] Shapes" in steel.

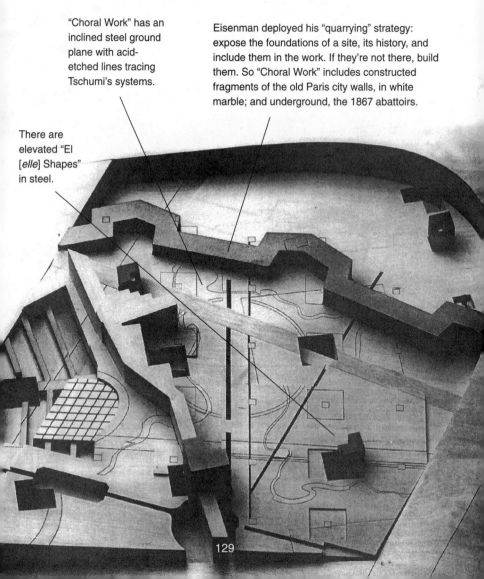

The exchanges raised important questions for both architecture and philosophy.

Could Eisenman's scheme "de-ontologize" the space as much as Derrida desired?

On the other hand, was such a philosophical move even possible for an architect, condemned – if building is to be done – to deal with materials open to certain notions of presence?

JACQUES WAS ONLY INTERESTED IN HIS LEXICON.

Other, external forces were at work. Scheduled for commencement in March 1987, "Choral Work" has not been built.

I'M NOT SURE IT WILL EVER BE BUILT. IT CAME OUT WAY OVER BUDGET AND THE CLIENT GOT FRIGHTENED. IT'S A TINY SITE, 70FT X 90FT, AND MOST OF IT UNDERGROUND...

IT'S A CRITIQUE OF EVERYTHING THAT SUBORDINATED ARCHITECTURE TO SOMETHING ELSE: *USE*, *BEAUTY*, OR *LIVING*. WE HAVE TO REFUSE THE HEGEMONY OF *FUNCTIONALITY*, OF THE *AESTHETIC*, AND OF *DWELLING*. IT'S A MOVE TO FREE ARCHITECTURE FROM ALL THOSE EXTERNAL FINALITIES, THOSE EXTRANEOUS GOALS.

For Derrida, a deconstructive architecture has to engage these forces. It means interrogating architecture's "traditional sanctions": that buildings should be USEFUL, BEAUTIFUL, and INHABITABLE.

This might suggest a wilfully useless, non-functional, uninhabitable, perhaps reckless, architecture. But *re-inscriptions* are possible...

Sanctions and Functions

Architecture cannot escape external forces: economic, political, legal, institutional, etc. "Choral Work" was no exception, if a little freer of them than usual.

Re-inscription

Beauty, usefulness, and functionality might occur, but
re-inscribed in the building. The external constraints and
finalities will remain, but subject to a deforming play.

This is the same tactic Derrida had used in *Glas*. Don't try to
refuse or reject edges, authors, title etc., but re-inscribe them in
ways that don't allow their usual, comfortable operation. It might
work in architecture.

Such an architecture will have to work through some powerful
"sanctions" of capitalist economics, industry, politics, as well as
ingrained notions of technical efficiency and habitability. In
architecture, deconstruction faces some of its most difficult
challenges.

And the inhabitants of the 19th *Arrondissement*? They live near
a large park, an object of international architectural curiosity.
And some architectural philosophy, some architectural
assumptions, have perhaps been challenged.

Postmodernism

Is deconstructive architecture *postmodern*?

Deconstruction has often been pulled into the orbits of postmodern culture or post-structuralist theory. But Derrida has resisted the prefix "post".

Deconstruction doesn't belong to an epoch or a period. Deconstructive moves might have features of postmodernism, or of modernism. But their main concern is to make alterations in the foundational groundings of cultural practices, whether classical, modern, postmodern, etc.

So it would be possible to *read* a deconstructive building through the themes of postmodernism (pluralism, heterogeneity, retro-style, etc). But it could also be given a deconstructive reading, one which sought out its potential for disrupting architectural and philosophical assumptions.

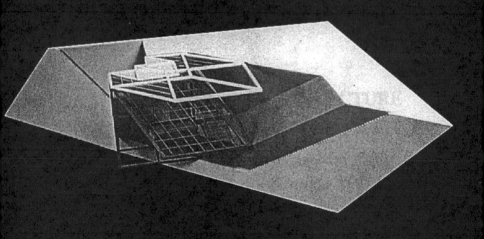

Likewise, perhaps, with art ...

THE VISUAL ARTS

Art critics and historians have applied deconstructive thinking to visual art. For instance, Sarat Maharaj finds a deconstructive play in **Pop Art**. Pop Art imports "found" popular objects and images into art. Are they readable then as popular culture or as art? Maharaj reads them as *pharmakons*.

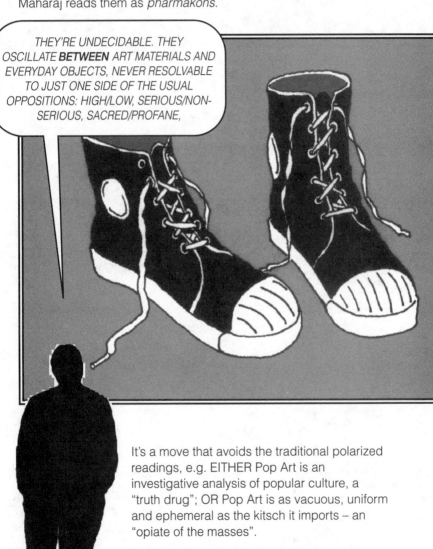

*THEY'RE UNDECIDABLE. THEY OSCILLATE **BETWEEN** ART MATERIALS AND EVERYDAY OBJECTS, NEVER RESOLVABLE TO JUST ONE SIDE OF THE USUAL OPPOSITIONS: HIGH/LOW, SERIOUS/NON-SERIOUS, SACRED/PROFANE,*

It's a move that avoids the traditional polarized readings, e.g. EITHER Pop Art is an investigative analysis of popular culture, a "truth drug"; OR Pop Art is as vacuous, uniform and ephemeral as the kitsch it imports – an "opiate of the masses".

If we treat its objects as undecidable, we're disturbing the oppositional distinctions on which these polarized readings are founded.

Jasper Johns

Art historian Fred Orton has suggested that works by **Jasper Johns** (b. 1930) might be read in deconstructive ways. For instance, Johns' titles often lie between the works they seem to name, and other works. "Passage" (1962) also names Hart Crane's poem "Passage". "Between the Clock and the Bed" (1981) also names the Norwegian artist Edvard Munch's "Between the Clock and the Bed".

These titles operate like *hinges* (Derrida's term "*brisure*"), bringing together and yet separating what is hinged, operating across a divide yet never belonging entirely to either side.

Johns' 1973 "Untitled (Skull)" is signed, as an art work properly should be, but the signature is crossed out, put under erasure.

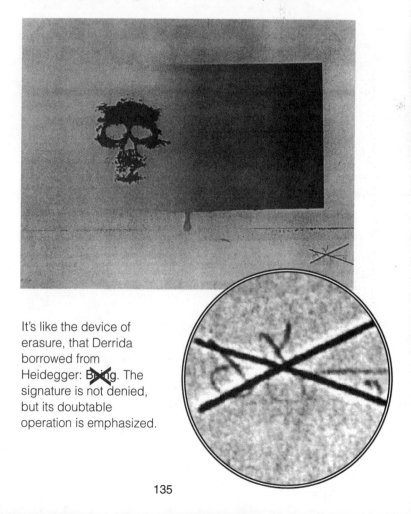

It's like the device of erasure, that Derrida borrowed from Heidegger: B̶e̶i̶n̶g̶. The signature is not denied, but its doubtable operation is emphasized.

The Truth in Painting

So the visual arts might use deconstructive strategies, in any epoch, and maybe without the name.

What about Derrida's contributions? He's written several times around art, especially in *The Truth in Painting* (1978).

Some of these essays examine contemporary art. Derrida writes diaristically around Titus-Carmel's diaristically-produced "Pocket-Size Tlingit Coffin". And he explores Valerio Adami's "Drawings After *Glas*", echoing Adami's use of fragmented, scarcely phonetic symbols – gl, cl, tr, +R: decomposed language.

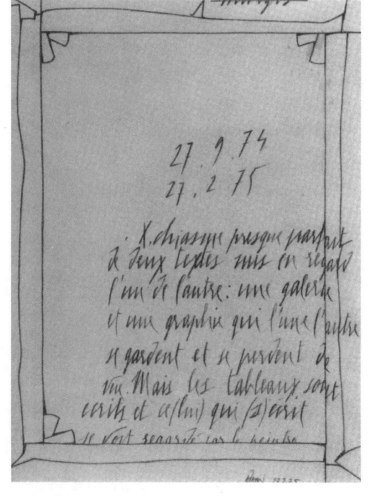

Study for a Drawing after Glas by Valerio Adami

But Derrida's main interests have been the nature of discourse about art – how written words might relate to visual artefacts. He's also asked how and why aesthetics has come to operate as a central field of concern for philosophy.

Kant's Aesthetics

Derrida takes up the question of aesthetics in a reading of
Immanuel Kant's *Critique of Judgement* (1790). It's a major work
of modern aesthetics – the philosophical field that asks what art
is, how it can be experienced, and how it can be judged or
evaluated.

Immanuel Kant 1724-1804

Kant lays out his analysis on the basis of an *opposition*:
pure reason/practical reason

This entails other distinctions:
sensible/supersensible
understanding/reason

And especially at stake are:
object/subject
nature/mind

For Kant, the problem was to bridge or resolve these
oppositions. Aesthetic judgement seemed to do that.
But Derrida shows how Kant used his notion of the
aesthetic to *conceal the impossibility* of doing it.

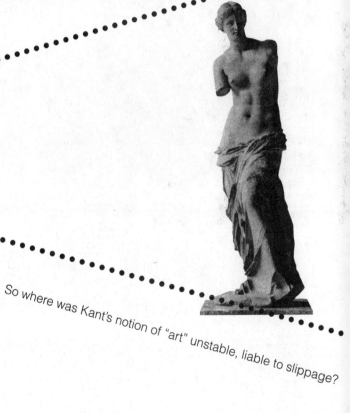

So where was Kant's notion of "art" unstable, liable to slippage?

Inside/Outside

Kant's "aesthetic object" has to have **intrinsic** beauty, value and meaning. This has to be distinguished from everything **extrinsic**, like its monetary value, circumstances of production or location, etc.

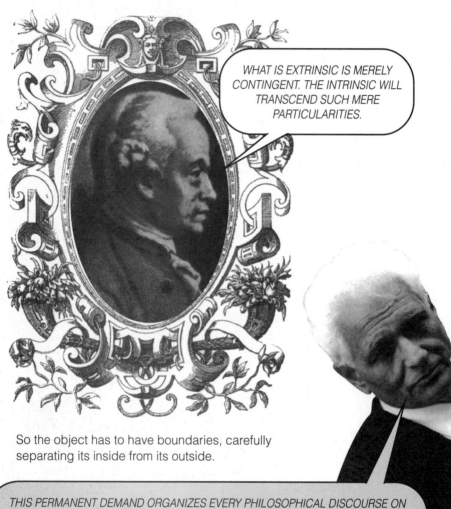

WHAT IS EXTRINSIC IS MERELY CONTINGENT. THE INTRINSIC WILL TRANSCEND SUCH MERE PARTICULARITIES.

So the object has to have boundaries, carefully separating its inside from its outside.

THIS PERMANENT DEMAND ORGANIZES EVERY PHILOSOPHICAL DISCOURSE ON ART, THE MEANING OF ART, AND MEANING ITSELF, FROM PLATO TO HEGEL, HUSSERL, AND HEIDEGGER. IT PRESUPPOSES A DISCOURSE ON THE **FRAME**.

Kant has to insist on the frame, enclosing and protecting an inside, while also creating an outside. This outside in turn has to be framed, and so on. It's the logic of the *parergon* (from the Greek "incidental" or "by-work") ...

The Parergon

In Kant's analysis, *parerga* are all those things attached to the work of art but not part of its intrinsic form or meaning. His examples: the frame of a painting, colonnades of palaces, drapery on statues. They're ornamental adjuncts.

They border the work but are not part of it. They resemble the work but are not identical with it. They belong to it but are subsidiary to it.

The *parergon* can be literally a picture frame, or some other adjunct to the work. Though the *parergon* encloses the work, brackets it, it also "communicates with the outside". It focusses or attracts attention to the work.

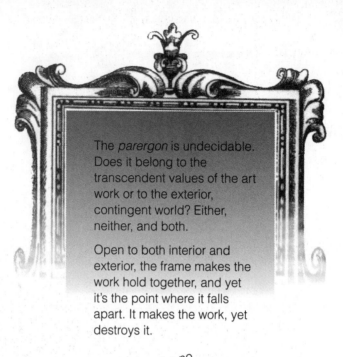

The *parergon* is undecidable. Does it belong to the transcendent values of the art work or to the exterior, contingent world? Either, neither, and both.

Open to both interior and exterior, the frame makes the work hold together, and yet it's the point where it falls apart. It makes the work, yet destroys it.

In spite of Kant's efforts, there can be no assured limits to the aesthetic object, telling us where to begin and end, where our attention *must* stop.

And if we can't be sure about the limits of the aesthetic object, categories like "aesthetic experience" and "aesthetic judgement" cannot be guaranteed. This is a problem for traditionalist Art History and a problem for philosophy. The oppositions of Kant's Enlightenment philosophy can't be bridged or resolved by appealing to art.

Mémoires d'Aveugles

The inside/outside opposition has also governed writing about art. What is inside art, therefore essential to art's identity, is what has to be written about. And the writing will be outside it.

Derrida has questioned this assumption. For instance in 1990 he curated for the Louvre, Paris, an exhibition of drawings and paintings – "Les Mémoires d'Aveugles" ("Memoirs/Memories of the Blind").

He treated the images as parergonal, as the permeable borders of his writing. It was a bid to bring attention to what is usually "exterior", and to set up passages across inside and outside, essential and inessential.

143

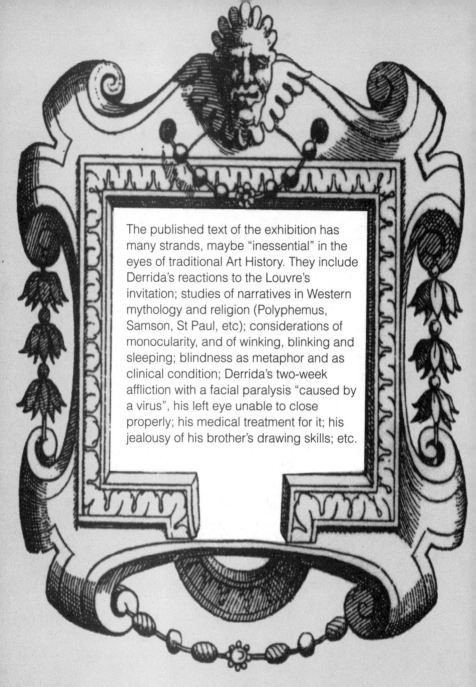

The published text of the exhibition has many strands, maybe "inessential" in the eyes of traditional Art History. They include Derrida's reactions to the Louvre's invitation; studies of narratives in Western mythology and religion (Polyphemus, Samson, St Paul, etc); considerations of monocularity, and of winking, blinking and sleeping; blindness as metaphor and as clinical condition; Derrida's two-week affliction with a facial paralysis "caused by a virus", his left eye unable to close properly; his medical treatment for it; his jealousy of his brother's drawing skills; etc.

Are these discourses *relevant*, are they *placeable* inside or outside?

Butades and the Début of Drawing

Derrida's exhibition opened up the interior of art in other ways. The figure of the artist has traditionally embodied the power and prerogative of seeing and making visible. But can art escape *blindness*?

The opening image of the exhibition was Joseph-Benoît Suvée's "Butades, or the Origin of Drawing" (1791), a painting of the young Corinthian woman Butades in Greek antiquity who, facing separation from her lover, traces his shadow on the wall.

*IT COMES FROM A TRADITION IN WHICH THE ORIGIN OF DRAWING IS ATTRIBUTED TO **MEMORY** RATHER THAN **PERCEPTION**. THE NARRATIVE RELATES THE ORIGIN OF GRAPHIC REPRESENTATION TO THE **ABSENCE** OR **INVISIBILITY** OF THE MODEL.*

And this suggests a blindness...

In Derrida's argument, drawing originates in blindness.

(a) The artist is blind...

While Butades traces, she cannot see her lover. She is blind to him as she draws.

The same goes for all drawing. The object or model, even if facing the artist, cannot be seen at the same moment as the mark of drawing is made. There's always a gap or delay. The mark relies on *memory*. And when memory is invoked, the present object is ignored: the artist will be blind to it.

(b) The process of drawing is blind...

Drawing, like language, is impossible without the play of the *trace*, the play of presence and absence. And this cannot be *seen*.

So there's a double blindness, with presence and absence (Butades' problem) at the origin. The artistic power of seeing and making visible is inhabited by blindnesses it cannot recognize.

So Derrida's writing on art, architecture and literature interrogates the foundational concepts of those fields, especially where they uphold the authority of Western philosophy. But his writing has raised many questions.

DOESN'T THE STRATEGY OF CONTAMINATION SIMPLY COLLAPSE TOGETHER ALL TYPES OF WRITING, ALL CULTURAL PRACTICES – FLATTENING EVERYTHING OUT?

This would collapse all differences into a generalized indifference. Philosophy, literature, art and other practices have their specificities, their particular demands and characteristics. These are important to recognize. Derrida has looked for *strategic* contaminations, at the points where metaphysical assumptions carry their greatest power.

ISN'T DERRIDA PROMOTING A KIND OF "TRANSCENDENTAL SOLIPSISM", DENYING "REALITY OUTSIDE THE TEXT"?

It's more a question of rethinking the usual, assumed relations between "reality" and "text". Appeals to "the real" are part of the foundational apparatus of Western thinking – for instance in philosophical positivisms, materialisms, etc. To deconstruct them is to leave no firm, clear line between concepts of reality and representation.

ISN'T DECONSTRUCTION A "NIHILISM", A PURELY NEGATIVE MOVEMENT THAT, FOR INSTANCE, DENIES THE POSSIBILITY OF MEANING OR OF POSITIVE ACTION IN THE WORLD?

Deconstruction does not deny meaning, but problematizes its usual assumptions. And for Derrida, deconstruction carries an affirmative impulse: "It entails affirmative action, linked to promises, involvement, responsibilities, commitment".

Deconstruction, therefore, has POLITICAL and ETHICAL implications.

POLITICS AND INSTITUTIONS

Derrida has addressed political issues in several ways.

First, his writing has raised questions **in general** of authority, of hierarchies, of law and right, and of language, communication and identities – philosophical questions with political implications.

But another strand of his work has been concerned with the politics of *institutions*. Philosophy must examine its own involvement in the transmission of knowledge and the politics of learning.

Derrida has played an active role in the organization GREPH (*Groupe de Recherche sur l'Enseignement Philosophique*), set up in 1974. GREPH challenged the traditional practices of French philosophy, but also campaigned against government plans to curtail the teaching of philosophy. It was a paradoxical project: to change philosophy, while calling for its maintenance, especially in schools.

In 1983, Derrida helped establish the government-sponsored Collège International de Philosophie, and became its first Director.

Platformed by GREPH, the Collège promoted new forms of philosophical activity. It supported interdisciplinary studies, research without pre-established goals or projects, the involvement of school teachers, and creative, performative interaction with architects, musicians, artists ...

I WOULD INSIST ON THIS OTHER DIMENSION – NOT ONLY PHILOSOPHY, BUT ACTIVITIES WHICH RESIST PHILOSOPHY AND PROVOKE PHILOSOPHY INTO NEW MOVES, A NEW SPACE IN WHICH PHILOSOPHY DOES NOT RECOGNIZE ITSELF.

ARCHITECTURE

POLITICS

PHILOSOPHY

THE ARTS

Writing Around Politics

Derrida has also engaged with "political" writing and activities in a wider sense.

He's undertaken the deconstruction of political texts and ideas. For example:

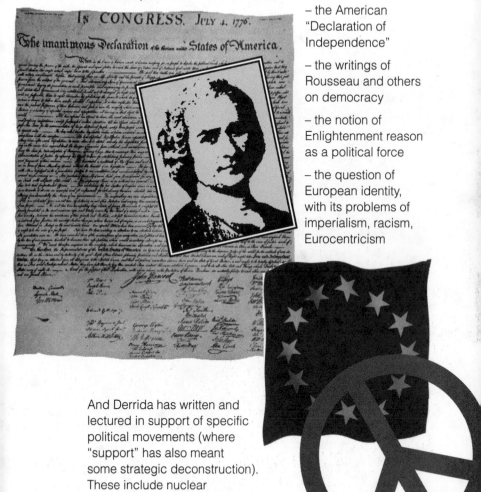

– the American "Declaration of Independence"

– the writings of Rousseau and others on democracy

– the notion of Enlightenment reason as a political force

– the question of European identity, with its problems of imperialism, racism, Eurocentricism

And Derrida has written and lectured in support of specific political movements (where "support" has also meant some strategic deconstruction). These include nuclear disarmament and the discourse of "deterrence", and the movement for racial emancipation in South Africa.

But the politics of deconstruction is a vexed question...

Alignments and Allegiances

Deconstruction might seem "revolutionary", but Derrida has questioned this. Revolutionary thinking is *teleological*. It proceeds *from* an origin *towards* a goal: a metaphysical procedure. Its aim is to overturn social and political hierarchies. This might be welcomed, but Derrida's main interest has been *displacement* rather than overturning.

> THERE'S ALWAYS A CONSERVATIVE CAST AVAILABLE TO IT.

Deconstruction resists alignment. It resists definition in terms of *programmes* or *positions*, of Left or Right, etc. In Derrida's view there is no programme. Each act has to have its programme made anew.

If deconstruction takes on responsibilities of a political nature, it shouldn't forfeit its interrogative vigilance: "Deconstruction should seek a new investigation of responsibility, questioning the codes inherited from ethics and politics."

Inevitably, deconstruction has been seen as politically protean, available to conservative, liberal, left or emancipatory tendencies. In the late 1980s, two controversies focussed attention on these issues.

The Heidegger Disputes

Derrida has often acknowledged his intellectual debt to Martin Heidegger, though he saw his own work as a departure from it – a *questioning* of Heidegger's concepts of origin, propriety, time and, especially, presence.

HEIDEGGER'S WORK IS EXTREMELY IMPORTANT TO ME, AND IT CONSTITUTES A NOVEL, IRREVERSIBLE ADVANCE, ALL OF WHOSE CRITICAL RESOURCES WE ARE FAR FROM HAVING EXPLOITED.

But it had long been known that Heidegger supported German fascism and its social trajectories, what he called the "inner truth and greatness of this movement (namely, the encounter between global technology and modern man)".

The facts were re-publicized along with new research in 1987. Victor Farias and others argued that Heidegger's involvement was a deep-rooted and long-standing commitment, not a temporary career compromise.

Heidegger was appointed Rector of Freiburg University in 1933, in the early years of Hitler's National Socialist government. He joined the party. His first administrative moves dismantled the democratic structures of the University, and his inaugural address encouraged the students to "sacrifice themselves for the salvation of our nation's essential being and the increase of its innermost strength in its polity."

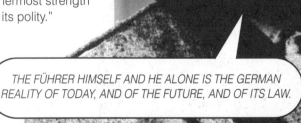

THE FÜHRER HIMSELF AND HE ALONE IS THE GERMAN REALITY OF TODAY, AND OF THE FUTURE, AND OF ITS LAW.

So was Heidegger offering a philosophy that matched the political trajectory of fascism? That's been the reading of many critics; for instance, Peter Osborne: *"He adopted the self-styled role of philosophical saviour of Germany. He offered Hitler a conservative revolution in philosophy: a mapping of ex-Catholic Christian **Geist**, Husserl's hermeneutics and modernist revolution."*

Derrida has suggested that there's more to Heidegger's philosophy than the German ideology of the period between the two wars.

INSINUATED "ANTI-SEMITISM" SHOULD NOT BE THOUGHT TO PASS OVER, BY "ATMOSPHERIC CONTAGION", TO ANYONE WHO DALLIES WITH AN ATTENTIVE READING OF HEIDEGGER.

Effectively, Heidegger's philosophy is defended over his politics.

The Paul de Man Controversy

Paul de Man (1919-83) was a leading North American proponent of deconstruction, a highly respected academic and teacher, and a friend and colleague of Derrida at Yale. In 1987 it was discovered that de Man had written wartime articles which supported the fascist government of German-occupied Belgium.

As a journalist in the early 1940s, de Man wrote for *Le Soir*, then controlled by the Nazis. Some of the articles argued, for instance, that Jews had "polluted" contemporary literature, that a "Jewish colony isolated from Europe would entail no deplorable consequences for the literary life of the West", and called for collaboration with the fascist government in a "common task" of the Belgian and German peoples. Five months after the passing of anti-Jewish laws, de Man wrote of the "impeccable behaviour of a highly civilized invader".

De Man emigrated to the USA in 1947, concealing his past. When he died in 1983, Derrida delivered a funeral address. He published memorial lectures in 1986 and a defence of de Man in 1988.

A vitriolic debate followed the revelations. Critics put at stake not only the authority and credibility of Paul de Man and his work, but also that of deconstruction.

The debates were complex, but two main questions arose.

First, was de Man's wartime journalism connected to his deconstructive literary theory – and if so, in what ways? Critics were divided...

Christopher Norris: "The later work can be read as a silent, reparative *undoing* of the earlier – as in de Man's horror of totalities, teleologies, 'immediatist' doctrines, and absolute truth claims."

Terry Eagleton: "Calling it a 'continuation of fascism under another name' is reckless hyperbole. But there is a continuity, though, in de Man's resolute opposition to emancipatory politics. The early extreme right-wingism mutates into a jaded liberal scepticism about the efficacy of any form of radical political action."

The other important question was how de Man's journalism could be read. Derrida explored the possibilities in his 1988 essay, "Like the Sound of the Sea Deep Within a Shell".

Derrida acknowledged that de Man's texts had an overall, dominant effect. Most often, they worked in conformity with the official Nazi rhetoric. [Derrida]: "There *is* an unpardonable violence and confusion in these texts."

But perhaps this overall effect was not consistent. De Man had supported modernist writers like Kafka, Gide, D.H. Lawrence and Ernest Hemingway. Their projects and texts were antipathetic to Nazism. And Kafka was Jewish.

Derrida found further inconsistencies. In one article, de Man begins by *criticizing* "vulgar" anti-semitism. Of course, he might have been implying that there's a "distinguished" variety. But he doesn't mention any.

THE PHRASE CAN ALSO MEAN SOMETHING ELSE, AND THIS READING CAN ALWAYS CONTAMINATE THE OTHER IN A CLANDESTINE FASHION: TO CONDEMN "VULGAR ANTI-SEMITISM", **ESPECIALLY IF ONE MAKES NO MENTION OF THE OTHER KIND**, IS TO CONDEMN ANTI-SEMITISM ITSELF **INASMUCH** AS IT IS VULGAR.

'VULGAR ANTISEMITISM'

Vulgarity Antisemitism

OR

Vulgarity Antisemitism

DE MAN DOES NOT SAY THAT EITHER.
IF THAT IS WHAT HE THOUGHT,
A POSSIBILITY I WILL NEVER EXCLUDE,
HE COULD NOT SAY SO CLEARLY IN THAT
CONTEXT.

n's article had been printed alongside other, notably
" anti-semitic articles. [Derrida]: 'These coincide, in their
lary and logic, with the very thing that de Man accuses,
s article were denouncing the neighbouring articles.'

ading of considerable subtlety. Derrida adds to it a further
n. Wasn't the villification of de Man reminiscent of the
ing, eradicating mentalities of fascism?

PdM   JD

TO CALL FOR CLOSING HIS BOOKS – THAT IS
TO SAY, AT LEAST FIGURATIVELY, FOR
CENSURING OR BURNING THEM – IS TO
REPRODUCE THE EXTERMINATING GESTURE
WHICH ONE ACCUSES DE MAN OF NOT HAVING
ARMED HIMSELF AGAINST SOONER.

a's most ardent critics objected to this logic.

agleton: "It makes de Man into the victim, rather than
n Jews. And it displaces the whole issue onto the malice
Man's critics: *they* are the true totalitarians. That's shabby
try."

re's more to deconstructive politics than this suggests...

Deconstruction and Feminism

How might deconstruction relate to practical, contemporary political struggles?

In the interview "Choreographies" (1982), Derrida suggests some possibilities. The politics in question are feminist, and deconstruction has no simple alliance with them...

To some ("difference") feminists, deconstruction has seemed useful. To put it simply, it works to dislocate categories like male/female or masculine/feminine: the foundations of patriarchal sexuality.

DECONSTRUCTION

PATRIARCHY

Other feminists (e.g. "equality" feminists) have seen it as a deflection or appropriation of feminism. Refusing clear political allegiances, deconstruction offers no grounds for feminist political action. It's the latest weapon in the male philosophers' armoury...

DECONSTRUCTION

FEMINISM

At first look, some of Derrida's arguments support the latter view. He has at times insisted on the estrangement of deconstruction from feminism.

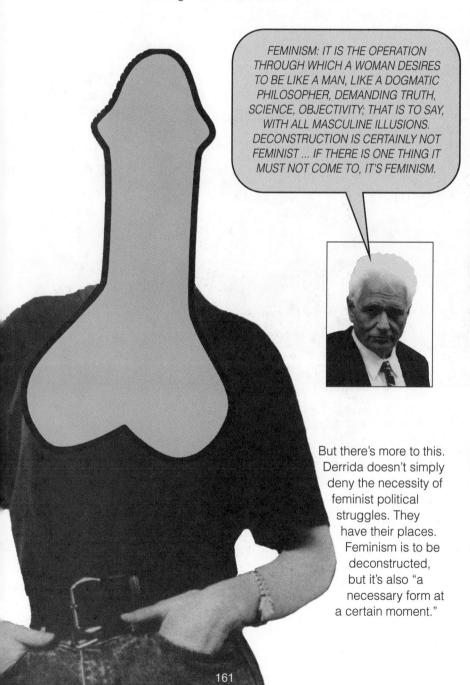

FEMINISM: IT IS THE OPERATION THROUGH WHICH A WOMAN DESIRES TO BE LIKE A MAN, LIKE A DOGMATIC PHILOSOPHER, DEMANDING TRUTH, SCIENCE, OBJECTIVITY; THAT IS TO SAY, WITH ALL MASCULINE ILLUSIONS. DECONSTRUCTION IS CERTAINLY NOT FEMINIST ... IF THERE IS ONE THING IT MUST NOT COME TO, IT'S FEMINISM.

But there's more to this. Derrida doesn't simply deny the necessity of feminist political struggles. They have their places. Feminism is to be deconstructed, but it's also "a necessary form at a certain moment."

Choreographies

In the interview "Choriographies", Derrida's interviewer invoked the figure of **Emma Goldman** (1869-1940), a "maverick feminist from the 19th century":

IF I CAN'T DANCE I DON'T WANT TO BE PART OF YOUR REVOLUTION.

Dancing and revolutions: Derrida's interest was the mismatching of their steps.

"Your maverick feminist showed herself ready to break with the most authorized, the most dogmatic form of consensus, one that claims to speak out in the name of 'revolution' and 'history'..."

Derrida suggests, against the protocols of "organized" revolutionary movements with historically conceived pre-ordained goals, a completely other history...

"...a history of paradoxical laws, of unheard of and incalculable sexual differences; a history of women who have 'gone further' by stepping back with their lone dance, or who are today inventing sexual idioms at a distance from the main forum of feminist activity – while still being able to subscribe to it, or occasionally becoming a militant for it."

Implicitly, the step back and the dance are deconstructive. Against this, revolutionary feminism is REACTIVE.

Derrida takes the term from **Friedrich Nietzsche** (1844-1900).

REACTIVE FORCES ARE UTILITARIAN, MERELY ADAPTIVE, AND SELF-LIMITING. ACTIVE, SUBJUGATING FORCES WILL PLAY TO THEIR LIMIT, ASSERTING THEIR DIFFERENCE AND MAKING THEIR DIFFERENCE AN OBJECT OF ENJOYMENT AND AFFIRMATION.

REACTIVE feminism, engaged in organized struggles, has to deal with the usual everyday language and practices of economics, law, rights, the media, etc. It has to accept metaphysical presuppositions and groundings. ACTIVE forces are a dancing. Derrida recognises the difficulty: "The most serious difficulty is the necessity of bringing the dance and its tempo into tune with the revolution. The madness of the dance can also compromise the political chances of feminism and serve as an alibi for deserting organized, patient, laborious feminist struggles, facing all the forms of resistance that a dance movement cannot dispel."

What then to do? Derrida doesn't suggest that reactive feminism should be combatted head-on. But it might be prevented from occupying the entire field, from becoming "what feminism is".

> YOU CAN SEE THE KIND OF IMPOSSIBLE AND NECESSARY COMPROMISE THAT I'M ALLUDING TO: AN INCESSANT, DAILY NEGOTIATION – INDIVIDUAL OR NOT – SOMETIMES MICROSCOPIC, SOMETIMES PUNCTUATED BY A POKER-LIKE GAMBLE, ALWAYS DEPRIVED OF INSURANCE...

So the necessity of deconstruction, as Derrida sees it, and the necessity of organized, goal-oriented struggles, are in *constant negotiation*. That's a problem for all organized political movements, where deconstruction is concerned.

Marx and Marxisms

Can the "dance" hold any weight against the need for emancipatory political revolutions? Derrida's engagement with Marxism in 1993 was greeted with interest. It's been seen as part of an "ethical turn" in deconstruction.

It was also said to be long overdue. Derrida had had some debating contacts with the Marxist *Tel Quel* group in the 1960s, and had been a friend and colleague of **Louis Althusser**, leading French Marxist-structuralist philosopher, at the École Normale Supérieure. Derrida found useful his attempts to free Marxism from Hegel's teleological thinking.

Derrida kept a relative silence on Marxism for the following 25 years. The machines of dogma, he says, were still at work.

It was perhaps a tactical silence. To deconstruct Marxism might have made Derrida complicit with the anti-communist Right of the Cold War.

Spectres of Marx

With the fall of communist governments in Eastern Europe in 1989, Derrida turned back to the question of Marxism.

Spectres of Marx (1993) suggests that deconstruction faced two opposing forces...

> *I OPPOSED, TO BE SURE, **DE FACTO** "MARXISM" OR "COMMUNISM" (THE SOVIET UNION, THE INTERNATIONAL OF COMMUNIST PARTIES, AND EVERYTHING THAT RESULTED FROM THEM).*

On another hand, another opponent: the New Right of neo-liberal Western democracies. Derrida opposed the political Right in its "manic triumphalism" over the collapse of communism. It's a dogmatic discourse, bidding for dominance, incapable of recognizing that the horizons of capitalism and liberalism "have never been as dark, threatening, and threatened".

So against the smug complacency of the New Right and Social Democracy, Derrida offers a list of indictments of contemporary global capitalism. It's a depressing picture of increased human misery, and Derrida places the blame in much the same quarters as most Marxists have done.

What's left of **Karl Marx** (1818-83)? Derrida resurrects him, but in *ghostly* form. He displaces Marx's realist ontology, the idea of a past or a present reality knowable without the "spectres" of its own making. In Marx's writing, there's a flight from the notion of "spirit". And for Derrida, the spirit is important – it shouldn't be denied or exorcized.

*IT OCCUPIES THE SPACE OF POSSIBILITY **BETWEEN** ABSTRACT IDEALS AND ATTEMPTS TO EMBODY THEM IN FULL "PRESENT" ACTUALITY. INSTEAD OF ONTOLOGY, "HAUNTOLOGY" – THE LOGIC OF THE SPECTRE.*

And for Derrida the emancipatory promise of Marxism is to be worked out in a new concept of justice. "It is perhaps even the formality of a structural messianism, a messianism without religion, even a messianic without messianism, an idea of justice..."

Marxist critics welcomed Derrida's principled stance on capitalism, and the placement of Marxism firmly on the agenda. And most complained that there was too little left of Marxism to offer useful, calculated resistances to state power and global capitalist economics. The debate continues.

So theorists and philosophers who have wanted to use deconstruction *and* other approaches have found it difficult. But some have done this – for instance **Gayatri Spivak**, English translator of Derrida's *Of Grammatology*. In 1990 Spivak was interviewed for the journal *Radical Philosophy*.

YOU'VE DESCRIBED YOURSELF AS A "PRACTICAL DECONSTRUCTIVIST FEMINIST MARXIST". WHAT KIND OF RELATION DO YOU SEE BETWEEN THESE?

THERE ISN'T ANY **COHERENCE** *– THE RELATIONSHIP IS MUCH MORE INTERESTING THAN A MERE COHERENCE. MARXISM LOOKS AT HOW CAPITAL OPERATES, FEMINISM HAS TO DO WITH THEORIES OF THE SUBJECT, SOCIAL PRACTICES OF SEXUAL DIFFERENCE. AS FOR DECONSTRUCTION: IT'S REALLY THE NAME OF A WAY OF DOING THESE TWO THINGS – OR ANY KIND OF THING.*

SO ONE COULD BE A DECONSTRUCTIVE CONSERVATIVE, FOR EXAMPLE?

I BELIEVE SO.

DID YOU LEARN THE DECONSTRUCTIVE APPROACH AND THEN GO ON TO APPLY IT IN PARTICULAR PROJECTS?

I DON'T THINK SO. FOR A TIME I FELT FEROCIOUSLY ANGRY WITH DECONSTRUCTION BECAUSE DERRIDA SEEMED NOT TO BE ENOUGH OF A MARXIST. HE ALSO SEEMED TO BE A SEXIST. BUT THAT'S BECAUSE I WAS WANTING DECONSTRUCTION TO BE WHAT IT ISN'T. I'VE REALIZED ITS VALUE BY RECOGNIZING ITS LIMITS – BY NOT ASKING IT TO DO EVERYTHING FOR ME... I HAVE VERY LITTLE PATIENCE WITH PEOPLE WHO ARE SO DEEPLY INTO DECONSTRUCTION THAT THEY HAVE NOTHING ELSE SUBSTANTIVE TO THINK ABOUT.

Deconstruction's Last Word?

These political debates have suggested that deconstruction, if it's to have an **ethical** commitment, must accept the necessity of grounded values which might well be un-deconstructable. That's been a major question for deconstruction in recent years.

There's much at stake in this, and in the fortunes and adventures of deconstruction in general. Put to use in wider fields, as Derrida has done, it's *more* than a "play with language", even though it insists that politics, ethics, economics, and law cannot *neglect* the play of language.

So what of the futures for deconstruction?

The death of deconstruction has been pronounced many times. It's a "passing fashion", a "momentary fad", it's "run out of steam", etc – a discourse similar to the funeral incantations around the death of Marxism, and perhaps just as misplaced.

To dismiss deconstruction in such ways is to reject too hastily the logic, however unfamiliar, of Derrida's writing. After all, deconstruction might *always* be at work. And that means that other movements, even if critical of deconstruction, will have to make themselves in fields already inhabited by it.

So: a future for deconstruction?

IT'S NECESSARY TO DISTINGUISH BETWEEN THE FATE OF THE WORD "DECONSTRUCTION", AND OTHER THINGS THAT ARE ABLE TO DEVELOP AS DECONSTRUCTION WITHOUT THE NAME. THE WORD WILL NOT BE USED INDEFINITELY. IT WILL WEAR ITSELF OUT. BUT BEYOND THE WORD, THIS MIGHT TAKE A LITTLE LONGER...

BIBLIOGRAPHY

Jacques Derrida is a prolific writer who's published to date more than 37 books and 250 essays, interviews, etc. The most complete list is by Albert Leventure, in David Wood (ed), **Derrida: a Critical Reader**, Blackwell, Oxford, 1992.

For further reading:
Christopher Norris, **Derrida**, Fontana, London, 1987.
Geoffrey Bennington & Jacques Derrida, **Jacques Derrida**, University of Chicago Press, 1993.

Collections of short texts and extracts are a good way of beginning to read Derrida's writing. See Peggy Kamuf's **A Derrida Reader**, Harvester, Hemel Hempstead, 1991, and Derek Attridge's **Acts of Literature**, Routledge, London, 1992.

Derrida's interviews are also useful. The most wide-ranging and best for beginners is **Points... Interviews, 1974-94**, ed. Elisabeth Weber, Stanford University Press, 1995. Earlier interviews are in **Positions** [1972], ed. Alan Bass, Athlone Press, London, 1987.

There are two useful collections on politics: **Institutions of Philosophy**, Harvard University Press, 1992, and **Negotiations: Writings**, Minnesota University Press, Minneapolis, 1992. See also **The Other Heading: Reflections on Today's Europe** [1991], Indiana University Press, Bloomington 1992.

For background reading to some of the debates...

The literary-critical debates are introduced in Christopher Norris' **Deconstruction: Theory and Practice**, Methuen, London, 1982, and Jonathan Culler's **On Deconstruction**, Routledge, London, 1983.

On deconstructive architecture, see **Deconstruction: Omnibus Volume**, ed. Andreas Papadakis et al, Academy Editions, London, 1989.

For art, see Peter Brunette and David Wills (eds), **Deconstruction in the Visual Arts**, Cambridge University Press, 1993. Two shorter accounts are in **What is Deconstruction?** by Andrew Benjamin and Christopher Norris, Academy Editions, London, 1989.

On gender politics and deconstruction, see Elisabeth Grosz's essay in **Feminist Knowledge: Critique and Construct**, ed. Sneja Gunew, Routledge, London 1990, and Diane Elam's **Feminism and Deconstruction: Ms. En Abyme**, Routledge, London, 1994.

Gayatri Spivak's writing is usefully introduced in **A Spivak Reader**, edited by Donna Landry and Gerald MacLean, Routledge, London, 1996.

For those who want to keep up to date, an annual review of what's been written on and about deconstruction is included in **The Year's Work in Critical and Cultural Theory**, Blackwell, Oxford, yearly from 1991.

Texts by Derrida:

'**Plato's Pharmacy**' in *Dissemination* [1972] Athlone Press, London, 1981.

'**Différance**' in *Speech and Phenomena* [1967] Northwest University Press, Illinois, 1973.

'**Structure, Sign, and Play in the Discourse of the Human Sciences**' in *Writing and Difference* [1967] University of Chicago Press, 1978.

'**Signature Event Context**' in *Margins of Philosophy* [1972] Harvester Press, Brighton, 1982.

Glas [1974] University of Nebraska Press, 1986.

'**Letter to a Japanese Friend**' [1983] in *A Derrida Reader*, ed. Kamuf (above).

'**Mallarmé**' [1974] in *Acts of Literature*, ed. Attridge (above).

'**Ulysses Gramophone: Hear Say Yes in Joyce**' [1987] in *Acts of Literature*, ed. Attridge (above).

'**Point de Folie - Maintenant l'Architecture**' [1986] in Bernard Tschumi, *Le Case Vide*, Architectural Association, London,1986.

The Truth in Painting [1978] University of Chicago Press, 1987.

Memoirs of the Blind [1990] University of Chicago Press, 1993.

'**Like the Sound of the Sea Deep Within a Shell: Paul de Man's War**' [1988] in revised edition of *Memoirs for Paul de Man*, Columbia University Press, 1989.

'**Choreographies**' [1982] in *Points... Interviews, 1974-94*, ed. Weber (above).

Specters of Marx [1993] Routledge, London, 1994.

Other references:

The 'matrix' statement [p.16] is from an interview with Peter Brunette and David Wills in *Deconstruction in the Visual Arts* (above). Derrida's comments on architecture [pp.124-5, 131] were made in interviews with Christopher Norris, *Architectural Design*, v59 n1-2, 1989, and Eva Meyer, *Domus*, v671, Apr 1986. Sarat Maharaj's 'Pop Art's Pharmacies' [p.134] is in *Art History* v15 n3, 1992, and Fred Orton's 'On *being* bent "blue"..' [p.135] in *Oxford Art Journal* v12 n1. Gayatri Spivak [pp.168-9] was interviewed for *Radical Philosophy*, n54, 1990.

Acknowledgements

The author and designer would like to thank all of the people who contributed to the preparation of this book. Without them, the task would have seemed more difficult and perhaps completely implausible. In particular, Jacques Derrida's generous and careful assistance was much appreciated, at an early and later stage of the production.

The designer would like to thank Andrea Levy, Judy Groves and Oscar Zarate for advice and help with research, and David King for permission to use images of Jean Genet and Emma Goldman derived from photos in his archive. Also, thanks to Ian Hooper and Nadina Al Jarrah for the kind loan of photographic equipment.

Biographies

Jeff Collins trained as a fine artist and studied art history at the University of Leeds. He is currently a lecturer in Art History at the University of Plymouth, and writes and lectures on contemporary culture and critical theory.

Bill Mayblin trained as a graphic designer at the Royal College of Art in London. He is the senior partner in the London-based design practice, Information Design Workshop.

Index

active vs. reactive 162–3
aesthetic judgement 139–42
Althusser, Louis 57, 165
anti-foundationalism 48
anti-Semitism 156–9
architecture 118–33
Aristotle 42
art 134–7
  and blindness 145–6
  exhibition 143–6
Austin, J.L. 80–3

Barthes, Roland 57
being, meaning of 49
Bennington, Geoff 93
binary opposition *see* opposition
blindness and art 145
boundaries questioned 12

Camus, Albert 98
chora 126–29
*Collège International de
  Philosophie* 150
communication 78–9, 85–90
  see also language; speech;
  writing
communism *see* Marxism
consciousness 51
constative utterances 80
contamination 100, 148
context 78–86

death vs. life 19–24
deconstruction 4–5, 7, 90–7
  architecture 118–28
  and feminism 160–4
  future 170–1
  implications 148
  Paul de Man 156–9
  politics 151–2
  postmodernism 133
  Gayatri Spivak 168–9
Derrida, Jacques
  background 13
  defended 10
  degree, honorary 6
  director of college 150
  opposition to 6–9

reading 15–16
thesis 14
who is he? 3
différance 75–7, 79

Eagleton, Terry 157, 159
Eisenman, Peter 119, 126–30
extrinsic value 140

fascism 153–5
feminism 160–4

Genet, Jean 112–14, 117
genre 115
Glas 111–17, 132
Goldman, Emma 162
GREPH 149, 150

Hartman, Geoffrey 116
Hegel, G.W.F. 112–13, 117
Heidegger, Martin 49, 56, 153–5
Hume, David 45
Husserl, Edmund 56, 60–1
Hyppolite, Jean 13

institutions 149
intelligible, the and *différance* 76
intention 86–7
intrinsic value 140
iterability and writing 83–9

Jakobson, Roman 57, 64
Jews and anti-Semitism 156–9
Johns, Jasper 135
Joyce, James 105–10

Kant, Immanuel 138–42

Lacan, Jacques 57
language 42, 78–83
  phenomenology 59–61
  Saussure 62–8
  serious/non-serious 82
  see also signified/signifier
Lévi-Strauss, Claude 57
life vs. death 19–24
literary criticism 111
literature and writing 98–102
logic 32
logocentrism 45